Mommy, Are We French Yet?

Mommy, are we French yet?

Shawn Underwood

five star
☆ ☆ ☆ ☆ ☆
misadventures

Seahurst, Washington

Five Star Misadventures, LLC
P. O. Box 1318
Seahurst, WA. 98062

www.ShawnUnderwood.com

Illustrations by Valerie Gower
Cover Design by Keli DeRitis
Book design by Jeanie James, Shorebird Media

Library of Congress Control Number: 2010925870

ISBN: 978-0-615-31652-9

PRINTED IN THE UNITED STATES OF AMERICA.

10 9 8 7 6 5 4 3 2 1

In Paris they simply stared when I spoke to them in French;
I never did succeed in making those idiots understand their language.
— Mark Twain

Boy, those French. They have a different word for everything.
— Steve Martin

Dedication

My heart-felt thanks go to:

My parents, John and Mary Ann Underwood. Their lust for life and spirit of adventure was my inspiration.

To my sister, Shannon, my "go to" person for stress relief, good laughs, and story line ideas.

To my publishing consultant, Jennifer McCord whose direction and encouragement made me see this book was indeed possible.

To Keli DeRitis, friend, website designer, and marketing consultant extraordinaire.

To my "office" support—the Starbucks baristas in Normandy Park, Washington, who encouraged me to see myself as a real writer.

To all my "peeps" (you know who you are), for your pep talks, brainstorming, walks, and generous, if often unsolicited, advice.

To my children, Austin, Conner, and Leslie, it's never too late to follow your dreams.

And finally, and most importantly, to my husband, Craig, who believed in me and kept my scattered work habits gently in check.

Prelude

Have you ever vacationed with your husband and children for an entire year? I'm here to tell you it can be done without killing each other.

Our (typical domestic) vacations usually start in a civil manner. We locate the rental car, check out the car for dings and dents, laugh about the roll down windows or the odd smell in the rent-a-wreck, and then drive out of the lot with the windshield wipers on instead of the lights.

Things invariably go bad when we have to navigate our way to a predestined vacation spot, or in one case, when we went to fill up the newly rented minivan.

"Shawn, unlock the gas cap, please," Craig said as he stomped from one foot to another in the biting cold.

"I can't find it, oh wait here it is, oops, there goes the hood," I said as I rolled down the window and quickly rolled it up again.

"Hurry up, it's cold out here. Oh never mind, I'll do it myself."

Of course the weather is foul, snow blows across the open hood of the car, and the wind whips Craig's coat open. I sit and watch from the comfort of the car and wait for the inevitable Craig storm.

"Shawn, for God's sake, unlock the car door, I'm freezing my butt off out here," said Craig.

Seeing my husband hunched over from the cold and pulling at the car door sends me into unwarranted hysteria—a very bad habit that occurs at the most inopportune times.

"I mean it Shawn, this isn't funny, unlock the #*#%& door right now."

And just like that, a perfectly good day has gone sour.

Now imagine if you were in a foreign country and the same scenario occurred. The car is an unfamiliar European brand, and the automobile manual is in French. Suddenly the simple task of opening the gas cap is magnified by a thousand, and now you have to talk to the attendant because your husband has refused to learn French. Then, there's the question of his manhood being challenged. Maybe the French gas station attendant will smirk at him. What man wouldn't know how to open the gas cap on his minivan? There's nothing to do but to muster up your limited French language skills and approach the intimidating fellow at the booth. Maybe he will help, maybe not. You never know with gas station attendants, no matter what part of the world you're in.

Was It The Wine Talking?

"We should all move to Europe in the next few years," said my husband, Craig.

"Why?" I said. My mother, father, sister, and brother-in-law awaited his answer as we sat at the dinner table.

"Why not? John, didn't you and Maryann say, and I quote, moving to Marbella was one of the best things you've ever done in your life?"

"Yes, I did say it, and it's still true," said my dad, John.

And so, the inception of moving abroad began. Because my parents had lived abroad with my younger sister, reinventing ourselves as ex-pats wasn't an unusual idea to us.

We're all fortunate in our jobs as commercial real estate developers, or a job some might term pavers of the planet. With Internet access, it was possible to run our business from abroad. We would be taking a year off in an off-year in real estate development. The timing was perfect. Wine-stained teeth and rose-colored glasses only increased our excitement for the possible upcoming overseas adventure. We began our research in earnest—to the astonishment of some of our friends.

Given the opportunity to live abroad for a year, leaving friends, family, fun-filled soccer games, Jif Peanut Butter, pet turtles, kids carpools, parent-teacher meetings, 24-hour access to most everything, would you do it?

Now, some people might say, "What, leave the country for a year? Betsy only likes Smith Brothers Milk on her cereal. I wonder if I can get Smith Brothers Milk in Europe? Where will the kids go to school and what about Ophelia's ballet class, she has that Christmas recital every year? I'd hate to miss it." Yes, that's what some people would say.

These same creatures of habit live in the same small town for their entire lives and have no inclination to venture out of their town, let alone their state, existing in a cocoon comfort of a one-story rambler—and I'm not saying it's a bad thing. Traveling via vicarious television viewing is enough for them. It's unthinkable to miss Ophelia's ballet recital.

I liken the idea of a year abroad to learning how to ride a horse. I wasn't exposed to horses early in life, except for one time my sister took me for a gentle ride on her horse, Bravo, and then slapped the hindquarters of said horse, leaving me to the mercy of the runaway nag. After that, I deeply mistrusted all horses; even a sawhorse left me weak in the knees. The fine steeds at the Emerald Downs racetrack thundering past at extreme speeds used to give me quite a fright. What if a wayward racing filly jumped over the fence off the track because of a delectable looking fake pansy decorating a spectator's hat? It could happen.

For me, horses were a risk, but living in another country for a year was only a matter of logistics—not a scary venture. My parents were rather unorthodox—they didn't let life pass them by. I remember being inoculated for various shots at a young age when it was decided we would all move to Pakistan where my father would work as a civil servant. They made it sound like such an adventure I was thrilled with the prospect of moving away, learning a new language, and making new friends. That trip didn't work out but the adventure seed was sown.

What made an impression on me as I made my way through my childhood years (besides a terrifying ride on Bravo the horse) was my parents' sense of adventure. Even procuring a pumpkin for Halloween was a risky venture in our household. Buying a pumpkin was out of the question.

"Dad, when are we going to go get a pumpkin?" I whined. "Don't worry, we'll go tonight, once it gets dark, oh and don't forget to wear your black ski hat and rubber boots," he said. He wasn't joking, and that made me nervous. He had the ability to make me quiver in my zorries, but mostly he was fun. His whistle proceeded him when he walked into a room, usually some "ahhh shucks, my horse got run over and died" sort of sorry, sappy song, my mom usually joined in harmony, and said she should have been a great opera singer. I'm not kidding. She did okay harmonizing with my dad but her version of Little Brown Owl left me wondering why the dog ran and hid under the couch. Whatever venture my dad cooked up, he had a willing partner in my mom.

That evening, I wondered why we were parking our beat up station wagon so far away from the "pumpkin patch." "Now, kids be very quiet and follow me," said my mom as she put on her black Pacific Trail ski coat, accessorized by a black jeweled belt and ski hat tilted at a rakish angle—one never knew who one might run into in a pumpkin patch. As we crawled along the ground amidst the giant pumpkins and slugs, my heart pounded in my ten-year-old chest. Why couldn't we have gone to the Safeway parking lot like the rest of the neighbors?

BANG—a loud report of a nearby farmer's shotgun, and I was up and running, as my parents yelled, "It's only a car backfiring, come pick out your pumpkin!" I cowered under our woody station wagon and waited for my younger siblings and my wretched parents to return. Looking out from under the car, I spied their mud-splattered boots, and then the thud of two giant pumpkins as they plopped down on the ground by the muddied feet. To this day, I don't know if the "pumpkin patch" was private (no trespassing) or the farmer was some high school friend of my father. Regardless, that night's outing made an impression on me and gave me a sense of adventure and daring and the ability to take risks, despite being terrified. A kernel was growing. Even then I wasn't destined to lead a safe, mundane life.

After I moved away to attend Washington State University, my parents and my younger sister, Shannon, left their fun, but still quiet suburban life and moved to Marbella, Spain for a year. Shannon seamlessly entered the Spanish culture, somehow her highly evolved sense of humor translated in Spain. Bright-eyed, with a winning smile and soft brown curls, she was an instant hit with the Spanish locals. A teen consulate-in-training. Her experience overseas gave us confidence that our children could excel as she did.

And so, in our forties and well into our careers, we decided to leave it all behind for a year. Shannon and her husband, Rick, were equally excited about planning and joining the upcoming venture, thus making our group a total of ten. My parents vacillated, they had a new boat and untested seas to explore.

∽ Part I ∽

Testing the Waters

Spain

Planning our year-long sabbatical actually preceded our trip abroad by two years. Our children, Austin (12), Conner (11), and Leslie (8) and their cousins, Kylie (7), Sean (5), and Kevin (2) remained unsure about the entire venture. Of course friends were all-important to them, friends that spoke English.

A year-long hiatus was a big endeavor, a new language, new food, new friends, and entering five of the six children into a new school. Our search for a country to live in was school-driven. It wasn't easy to find an International School with a good reputation in a desirable area that would accept five children.

So, we investigated possible countries, the most plausible was Spain. My husband, Craig, the type A personality of the group, was thorough and methodical in his research. Craig's mantra is "Craig's way is the RIGHT way." Fortunately, his witty comebacks and generous spirit softened his insistence on "Craig's way." Craig lobbied for Barcelona. "Barcelona has loads of schools to choose from and the culture is fabulous." It was true we all spoke a bit of Spanish, Shannon being the most fluent, although I later discovered her command of the Spanish language was a bit . . . halting. Shannon was a tad out of practice since her 1977 stay in Marbella, Spain.

We made the necessary appointments from home with the headmasters of the schools we wanted to visit, determined by Internet research and school location. Our primary concern was getting the kids into a good British-American school, if we were successful, we would look at houses to rent. We gave ourselves one week to "test the waters."

In the fall of 1999, our week-long foray started in Marbella on the Costa del Sol in Spain. Not only was the weather on Costa del Sol temperate, but there was a large ex-pat community. Having an English-speaking community was a huge bonus because my recollection of junior high school Spanish was hazy at best. I remember using "cue-sheets" at Highland Junior High School to learn Spanish. The "cue-sheets" were a cartoon style worksheet that depicted the family of Pepito and Emilio and their dog, Iman. "¿Dónde está Iman?" "Iman está aquí." "Voy a la nadar." Interpreted as, "Where is Iman?" (Iman is the dog.) "Here is Iman." And of course, the always-useful phrase, "I'm going swimming."

Most of the English-speaking private schools in Europe followed the British curriculum, which has a stellar reputation. Consensus of those living abroad was that the American curriculum encompassed reams of memorization and stacks of task-oriented worksheets and fill-in-the-blanks. Our on-line research indicated the British curriculum focused on a comprehensive approach to learning; for example; learning grammar specifics through reading and writing literature rather than circling a verb or making something plural in a worksheet. Certainly a different learning style than my children's parochial school education, however, I'm sure there are benefits to both styles of learning.

After we landed in Marbella, we drove several hours south for an appointment at the Sotogrande International School. The small town of Sotogrande was developed in the 1960s as a resort town because of the temperate climate and close proximity to the sea. It boasted a large marina, world-class golf courses and an International polo field. The neighborhood surrounding the golf course could have been any upper middle class neighborhood in the United States. Sotogrande was a multi-lingual community of German, English, and Danish expatriates seeking sun and a more relaxed atmosphere than what Marbella had to offer.

The headmaster of Sotogrande International School was a very effusive fellow although he had a tendency to jump from one subject to another at a rather alarming rate. "The Princes William and Harry were here last week at the International Polo game. One of them took a rather nasty spill but he turned out all right in the end," he said. "Will our kids have a chance to play polo?" I asked. I immediately envisioned Prince Harry helping my son, Conner, mount his pony, while I stood nearby and made idle chatter with Prince Charles. Craig (bursting my bubble) said most certainly our children wouldn't be playing polo, what was I blathering about and we still had other schools to tour.

The International School of Sotogrande met all of our requirements and they had room for all of the kids. The school not only had every sport imaginable for my active boys but they excelled in the arts and were in the process of completing a new campus. Three of us loved the school, but my sister, Shannon, was a bit worried it was too much like home.

After our quick overnight trip to Sotogrande, we drove north back towards Marbella. We had an appointment with the headmaster of Sunny View International School in Torremolinos. We drove by the dilapidated school in the shoddy neighborhood and the four of us mutually decided to skip the in-school tour, though none of us was brave enough to face down the headmistress and personally cancel the appointment. If her demeanor was anything like the school façade, we were sure to have an unpleasant appointment.

Somehow, I felt sure a missed appointment wasn't an unusual occurrence for her. The town of Torremolinos was less than desirable, and if the school was anything like the town, our children were doomed to a year in purgatory. It was late afternoon and too late to drive to our next stop, so we regretfully opted to stay in Torremolinos. We had no hotel reservations and it seemed as though the town was full.

We stayed at a roadside campground that posed as a hotel. Our double bed was rock hard and lumpy, the walls paper-thin, and the pool filled with vermin. A lot of unsavory-looking people wandered up and down the halls practicing Elvis songs in Spanish. British football (soccer) hooligans kicked an old soccer ball against the hallway walls during the night, which made it impossible to sleep. Much to our dismay, an Elvis impersonation contest enlivened the evening. We retired to our rooms, complete with dirty ashtrays and questionable bedding. All rooms were smoker-friendly which required immediate ventilation. We threw open the windows only to be serenaded with exceedingly bad Elvis impersonators. We slept on top of the beds with our flimsy towels and coats for cover and prayed for dawn. The following morning we picked our way through the cigarette and empty *cerveza* bottles that littered hallway.

Our next stop was The Almunecar International School near the town of Nerja. Nerja was about as far from civilization as one can get and still find a petrol station. Suffice it to say, there was no movie theatre or grocery store. As we drove through town, Shannon waxed enthusiastically about the tired-looking donkeys laden with pots and rugs. "Shannon, they are blocking the road and I bet you wouldn't like to constantly be dodging donkey piles along the street," I said. The ragged underwear and T-shirts strung on clothing lines from the few ramshackle apartment complexes really had Shannon's pioneer juices flowing. She impulsively shouted, "This is where my people live." This didn't surprise me. Shannon had a strong desire to live off the land and wash her clothing on river stones. Shannon can pretty much do anything and nothing would make her happier than to lead the kids on a cart horse to school every day from her home situated in a remote village with nothing but goats and sheep for company. She wouldn't want to miss out on living with "her people." She doesn't like to miss out on anything. Craig and I preferred at least a few modern conveniences, as did her husband, Rick. Even though the rest of us wanted to cancel our three o'clock appointment at the Almunecar School, Shannon wouldn't be deterred.

At the Almunecar School, the classes were taught following the British curriculum. In this case, the British accents failed to enchant me, the children in sixth grade were no less than dreadful. Just as we entered the classroom for introductions, a large unkempt boy tortured an equally massive youth with the teacher's eraser. I believe some crumbled chalk extended from the harassed youth's ear. The harried teacher ceased her fishwife yell as we entered the classroom. "Ahhh, here you see us, warts and all." We never made it past the doorway as she hastily retreated from the classroom and made some inept excuse for the children's unruly behavior. Despite being offered lunch, we left as quickly as we arrived, and crossed our fingers and toes for Sotogrande. Thus far, it was the only decent school that had room for our children.

When we returned home from Spain a week later, we filled out all of the necessary paperwork, complete with fetching photos of the children and emailed the forms to the Sotogrande headmaster

We eagerly awaited the three weeks the headmaster quoted us for our children's acceptance pending current grade and exam reviews. Our children's teacher recommendations simply glowed with praise for our young offspring. We were never entirely sure of the motivation behind these recommendations, because one of the kids was very familiar with the principal of the school.

Six months later we were still waiting for the kids' admission to Sotogrande School when my brother-in-law, Rick, and I began discussing the lackluster cuisine in Spain. We'd ordered fish at most restaurants. However, neither of us liked fish cooked in massive amounts of oil. As our digestive systems rebelled, we both lost weight and enthusiasm for the south of Spain, although we tempered this with *cervezas*. Rick is, by far, the most reasonable of the four of us. Growing up as a middle child in an Irish Catholic family with seven brothers and sisters, taught him the ability to see both sides of a situation. His chameleon demeanor often proved useful when dealing with my sister's improbable flights of fancy; in this case, living in Nerja, Spain at the end of a coast road with no access to a nearby airport. By unanimous decision, it was back to the drawing board. Reflecting on our exploratory journey, we realized that although the people exude warmth, the Costa del Sol had too few enticements, the schools have not panned out and we cannot live on *cervezas* and greasy fish alone. We were ready to begin research on another country in which to live.

One morning, as I read the *Seattle Times*, I stumbled across an interesting article. Columnist Jean Godden described her recent vacation in St. Paul du Vence in France. She extolled about the countryside, the food, wine, and of course the culture. She described it as heaven—paradise lost. After contacting the author via email and phone, I too was convinced of the merits of the south of France and determined, as my impulsive nature often dictates, to convince the others of the viability of southern France.

After scouring the Internet we found no schools in St. Paul du Vence, however, other villages within the area had a plethora of English-speaking schools and apparently quite the ex-pat community. We determined our next exploratory venture solely based upon Jean Godden's recommendation, Internet research, and the final enticement—a friend of a friend who lived there with her children.

Rick, Shannon, and Craig were equally enthused when they reviewed the school selection possibilities. Shannon had studied French for at least six years in school, and I had studied in Avignon, France, for three months with the semester exchange program at Washington State University. I knew enough French to ask directions, perhaps interpreting the answer will pose a problem, but I'd worry about that later. Shannon said she could ask for ketchup for her *frites*, the location of the toilet, and rent a small boat, if necessary. Rick and Craig were enthused, although Craig continued to lobby for Barcelona, Spain reasoning we needed to add more culture to our lives. He was right but still outvoted, three to one. Rick and I hadn't forgotten about the oily fish in the south of Spain.

We made the necessary appointments with the headmasters of the schools we wanted to visit, this solely determined by Internet research, school location, and our limited knowledge of the French language. We began planning our next overseas journey to scout for schools.

France

For the trip to France, we upgraded to Business Class and arrived in London much refreshed after a leisurely rest on British Airways. At one point, I was rather flummoxed when the flight attendant asked, "Would you like a slumber suit?" "Excuse me, what did you say, slumber what, do you mean pajamas?" I cautiously asked. She didn't catch me out again, even after she asked if I wanted some "biscuits" disguised as cookies.

Nine hours later, we arrived in Nice and wandered around the airport for more than an hour before we located the correct car rental agency. Our lack of language skills prevented us from communicating our problem, although Shannon did manage to ask a nearby café waitress for some ketchup.

After a few minutes, the rather stiff attendant at the agency directed us to a nearby booth where we rented a small mobile box posing as a car. "Rock-paper-scissors" designated Craig as the driver and we skirted our way inland to Valbonne, with Rick as the navigator. Craig and Rick together in the front seat insured zero yelling in the car; men don't yell (at each other) about bad directions and inept driving skills. According to the map, Valbonne was central to most of the International School locations.

There was some confusion in the vehicle about negotiating the roundabouts. A roundabout is one of the traffic systems used in France in place of a stoplight. It's a large two-lane circle, with four or five main exits off of the circle. It's very efficient for people who know how to use it. We didn't know how to use it or even what it was, therefore, problems ensued. Other drivers honked at us, and angry fists extended out a few car windows. Our husbands ignored all gestures and honks, while Shannon and I took cover in the backseat. We negotiated the large circle with the many exits as we drove round and round until we figured out the correct exit to dart out of. Shannon and I gaily chatted in the backseat as we were thrown about by Craig's rather erratic driving. Craig (type A) hadn't yet figured out he wasn't the master of the roundabouts—I'm sure it was very annoying for him.

Eventually, we came across the picturesque town of Valbonne. We definitely needed a break after the hectic drive, so we stopped for an espresso and *pain au chocolat,* a delicious croissant filled with two rows of dark chocolate. The sun warmed our backs as we sat in the extremely pleasant central plaza. I picked up a few French words from the locals sitting at a nearby table and felt I might "fit in." The sweet smell of the fresh cut roses on the flower cart in the plaza enticed my senses. An English-American bookstore inhabited a yellowed, old stone building. We were enchanted; convinced we had found our home away from home. Now, the real work began, we had to find a school with enough space for five of our six children.

We toured no less than nine schools in the area, only three of which impressed us. Our favorite school was in Mougin, France, conveniently close to our favorite town of Valbonne. The school was brand-new, had forms K-12, warm, caring, and friendly teachers and run under the British curriculum.

The headmaster of Mougin School was ninety percent sure all of our kids could start in the fall of 2001. We were, of course, overjoyed but cautious, remembering the lack of follow-through with the Sotogrande School in Spain. We decided that we needed a "back-up" school, so, we toured a few other schools over the next several days.

The International School of Nice was in the industrial district of Nice, a chain-link fence surrounded it, the playground was completely asphalt, there was no grass . . . anywhere. As we entered the school, we were dismayed to see that the upper school students seemed to be missing some of their clothing, a lot of skin was showing, some kids were smoking in the "smokers lounge" in the inner (at least outdoor) courtyard. The headmistress informed us The International School of Nice had room for all of the kids. The lower form grades appeared to be very well run, so at least three of the five kids would be in good hands if they attended the school. Another point to consider was the drive from Valbonne, we were all in love with country life as opposed to city dwelling and Valbonne was forty-five minutes one-way. However, since we did not yet have a house secured it was a moot point.

One other school in Mougin rated high on our list, the kids attending this school were from families of transitory workers stationed with French companies. However, we found out that the children attending the school must be proficient in French and English in order to qualify—an obvious problem for our kids, so we were down to two schools.

The Hunt for Houses

Before our exploratory venture to the south of France, we located a real estate agent through friends of friends. We had arranged a meeting prior to our arrival in France. Our agent, Maryann, was an ex-pat French/Canadian who now lived in Grasse. She was extremely thorough and understood the importance of locating rental homes close to the Mougin School. According to Maryann, there was no such thing as MLS or multiple house listings in the south of France, so it was important to work with an agent who had a lot of contacts and listings. We didn't have the luxury of time for twenty different agents to show us their individual listings. Maryann had a broad network of listings and, of course, spoke fluent English, a distinct advantage for us.

One of the first homes we toured was an old French chateau. We were all smitten, the antique iron gates opened up to a graveled drive surrounded by magnificent gardens. Yellowed stone and curved arches graced the house. Even in the dead of winter, the gardens retained their charm and the sun still held a bit of warmth as we waited outside for the owner.

Maryann told us that the owner was a Baroness from Germany. She had never rented her home however she was planning a year-long vacation beginning in the fall of 2001 and wasn't opposed to a little extra cash.

The dowager Baroness greeted all of us with a halting English accent at the massive front door. She wore her country tweeds and her sensible shoes clacked on the honey-colored pavers worn with age. A fire burned in the original stone fireplace, which was tall enough to walk through. Looking out the leaded-glass French doors, the city of Grasse and the valley were visible beyond the Olympic-sized pool.

The house was totally private, and within easy walking distance to the nearby village of Châteauneuf de Grasse. However, we hadn't seen the kitchen. The kitchen was not good, it was small, very, very small, and the minute refrigerator had no freezer. The oven had knobs and dials we didn't recognize; the range was French after all. There was no table in the kitchen, and where were the cupboards for the food?

The office was rather dated. A stilted conversation in French was exchanged between the stern Baroness and Maryann. Not to worry, the Baroness said there would be all new wiring, and the electrician would arrive within the month. The basement was dismal, there was no dryer, but this wasn't unusual because the French use outdoor clotheslines. A peculiar odor was emanating from the basement. The Baroness suddenly couldn't understand my sister's pigeon-French when she asked about the strange smell from the subterranean room. Upstairs, the master bedroom was large and airy; however, there was no shower, only some sort of handheld device used to spray the soap off one's head. The other bedrooms were very small but habitable.

The yard was the selling point. It was like a park with mounds of well-kept grass and olive trees scattered about. There was a clear view of the Grasse valley from the Olympic-sized pool, which was surrounded by stone pavers.

Despite these few drawbacks, we were sold; the only problem was to decide who would actually rent the house, Rick and Shannon or Craig and I?

Again, Maryann had a solution; there was another home, down the narrow pot-holed street from the glorious chateau. I could only describe it as a "rabbit warren." Shannon was of course enamored with the warren, it had so many hallways and doorways, we were immediately hopelessly lost when the owner took us on a tour. The rabbit warren septic system wasn't functioning as evidenced by the strong aroma in the expansive sparsely grassed yard. Some of the smell emanated inside but my sister wasn't deterred. Rick saw the telltale gleam in her eye, but refrained from commenting, I was sure they'd have words later. Shannon visualized her small children splashing in the pool. The rabbit warren had a massive pool with cushy lawn chairs surrounding the clear water. This was a very strong contrast to the foul outdoor odor. I wondered about the lack of wildlife in the area (the leaking septic system perhaps). The owner of the Rabbit Warren assured Shannon and Rick the broken septic system would be repaired before they took occupancy. Shannon turned very red in the face as she tried to say something in French about signing the lease immediately. She was desperate to live in the Rabbit Warren. Luckily, the owner failed to understand her and Rick forcibly dragged her out the door. I shuddered with dismay, and Rick glowered at Shannon's impulsive outburst. While the Rabbit Warren was quaint and held some charm, the overall disrepair of the house and grounds left me wondering about Shannon's enthusiasm. Because Shannon was eagerly following the homeowner, she wasn't witness to Rick's barely stifled laughter as we toured the house. Rick wasn't going down without a fight.

We left France, feeling we had accomplished what we had set out to do; we had options for two schools and two homes to rent—Shannon and Rick were going to rent the Rabbit Warren on a month by month basis. Phase One of our 2001-2002 venture was complete, all that remained was the paperwork, and of course, packing and closing up our homes for a year.

~ Part II ~

The Journey Begins

How Many Underpants Do I pack for a Year Abroad?

Exhausted from packing, I fall into bed at 12:30 for a few hours of sleep before the first leg of our journey begins tomorrow. Our year-long trip to France has been in the planning stages for months. My sister, Shannon, brother-in-law, Rick, and their three children, Kylie, Sean, and Kevin are our partners in this year-long venture. Our children, Austin, Conner, and Leslie are not quite as thrilled with the entire venture as Craig and I.

In preparation for the trip, Rick and I studied *French in 10 Minutes a Day* and placed French language stickies all over the house. Shannon preferred the more traditional study method. She enrolled at Bellevue Community College to "brush up" on her high school French. My husband, Craig, maintained that his junior high school Spanish would suffice as a second language and says, "Everyone speaks English."

Packing for an entire year away from home with three kids is a giant task. All the kids are heavily involved in sports, they have different shoes for each sport and their feet are still growing. Not knowing if our little corner of France would have sporting goods stores that carried kids' sport equipment, we packed Austin's cleats, bats, and baseball glove. We packed Leslie's ballet shoes, Conner's swim team goggles, and speed suits. Each person in our family was allotted two boxes, the box size being the maximum size allowed for luggage; a useful tip from the friend who introduced us to Maryann, the real-estate agent who secured our homes for us, nearly six months prior to our departure. Craig and I ended up with the beautiful French château, (Shannon and Rick lost the coveted château in a tense game of "rock-paper-scissors.") They are moving into a brand new home—sight unseen. The owners of the Rabbit Warren sold the house to some unsuspecting, smell-challenged American.

Our kids rose with minimal whining, a good start to a very long day of travel. The previous evening we loaded all ten of the tightly taped cardboard boxes into a friend's diesel truck. At 6:40 A.M. sharp, we pulled into our friend's driveway. Bleary-eyed but excited the kids handed off their carry-on luggage to our friend, who attempted to stuff the extra bags into his already overcrowded truck. At this rate, his wife would be jogging behind the truck. Problem solved, we drove two vehicles.

At the airport, the skycap reminded me of an over-anxious car salesman. He saw the two vehicles pull up and in his haste to help us, had his knees banged when I opened the passenger door. Craig believed the skycap had x-ray vision and could see the truck-cab filled with giant boxes and bags and perhaps a generous tip for his services. Regardless, the skycap was very helpful, and we were quite pleased not to have to wait in the long baggage line with the other disgruntled passengers.

Things were running smoothly until the ticket taker stopped the children with their carry-on bags. "Those bags are definitely too big. Put them in sizing bin up front." Too scared to argue with the troll, the kids complied as commanded. They had to check their bags, probably never to see them again. I at least have my smaller bag, which apparently is suitable as a carry on. The kids will have no school supplies, toothbrushes, or underwear. Craig manages to keep his cool when the kids flunk baggage carry on. It's my fault because I picked out the bags and packed them, and the bags resembled over-stuffed sausages. I believe that I heard only a very few choice words under

Craig's breath. I don't know why he cared, at least he had his toothbrush.

Sitting in the bulkhead wasn't too bad, close to the facilities and first in line for food. I sat between Thing 1 and Thing 2, Conner and Leslie respectively. This leg of the journey was painless; we had only to travel from Seattle to Detroit. Craig was peacefully typing on his laptop across the aisle; the sun hit his shoulder with what I imagine to be a lovely warmth. He paused in his writing and looked out the window, ever so calmly. Austin quietly sat beside him playing with his Game Boy, an excellent traveling companion when he is away from Thing 1 and Thing 2. The next leg of our journey was from Detroit to Rome, which would take about eight hours. Once in Rome, we had a one-hour flight to Nice, France.

Still on the flight to Rome, I was rudely awakened from my daydreaming when Leslie bumped Conner, who spilled his water all over the front of his neighbor's pants. The poor man looked as though he had a bad accident, but fortunately he was blissfully asleep.

I was in luck. It was Craig's turn to sit between Leslie and Conner, let him deal with Mr. Soggy Pants.

Touchdown: Nice, France

We arrived in Nice, France, our new home, after a minor delay in Rome. We did miss one flight, which required us to sprint through the airport to catch the next flight. I'm still amazed that the dapper attendant with the short legs could run so fast. I hustled after him dragging my carry-on suitcase, purse, wool coat, sweater, and sweatshirt. Early on in the trip, I tried to stuff my sweater and sweatshirt into Craig's luggage when he wasn't looking but one of the kids ratted on me. I tried to explain to Craig that my extra clothing was a precaution in case my baggage was lost. "Shawn, each person has two boxes, that should be enough even for you." I don't know what he meant by this statement. Our height-challenged flight attendant obviously knew what he was doing as all of our bags and boxes arrived in Nice on time.

Our real-estate agent, Maryann, was waiting for us at the Nice airport. She brought her gardeners with their big muscles and rake-filled truck to help us with all of our bags and boxes. The gardeners quickly loaded the luggage and drove away at a breakneck pace and we managed to follow them (after we located the car-rental agency) to the old château that we so fondly remembered.

Our picture-perfect château with the red tiled roof, magnificent old front door, and the massive iron knocker is just as we remember it. The neighborhood is charming; gates front all of the various properties, regardless of the state of the home. The chickens noisily run across the road as we drive down the pothole-filled street and old women with worn floral aprons point and stare at us. No one waves. Perhaps it's impolite to wave in France. It's an eclectic neighborhood, and the massive honeyed château that we are soon to occupy is most definitely the jewel of the area, or at least it appears to be from the outside.

After dropping us off, Maryann scurries out the door to pick up Rick and Shannon, her next stop—their brand-new home located conveniently down the road from us. The home was to be completed by the time they arrived according to the English owner. The builders said they just needed to complete a few items on the punch list.

Maryann hurriedly introduced me to the estate caretaker before she left for the airport. The caretaker lives in a small house on the expansive property. I can sort of understand the caretaker's French, but I'm a poor communicator at best. As she shows me how to operate the stove, I wonder out loud if I'm supposed to separate the garbage and recycle. Perhaps I miscommunicated because apparently recycling doesn't appear to exist in France, at least not today. I think she also said a painter starts work on September 15 on the inside of the house. I sincerely hope I misunderstood her French, because this isn't welcome news. The painting and the rewiring were supposed to be completed prior to our arrival.

As I wandered around the antiquated old manse, I began to have renter's remorse. What was I thinking? There is no real shower, no microwave, no disposal, a haphazard Internet connection, no television connection to English-speaking channels, and no clothes dryer. I silently curse myself for forgetting practicalities in my captivation with this antiquated manse. Of course, there's the fabulous estate-like park our rented home is situated on and the pool. Who needs all those American frivolities such as wiring and freshly painted walls? Hanging my laundry to dry on the outdoor clothesline will be a novel experience; I might even grow to like it.

I wondered aloud to Craig, "Do you think Rick and Shannon have arrived?"

Tired of unpacking, we ambled down the street to visit Rick and Shannon in their new house. We figured it wouldn't be too hard to find their new house with multitudes of construction workers scurrying about and putting the final touches on their new residence.

Their home sits atop a very steep graveled drive, I'm glad we are walking, and wonder about navigating the driveway in a vehicle. The new house is a shining star in the neighborhood of old crumbling homes and a few recently updated manses. The smell of fresh paint is evident as we walk inside and see the kids propped in front of the satellite television, our television has a grainy picture at best. Shannon and Rick invite us to sit by their currently unfinished pool amid the rubble as the construction workers drilled through the pool deck to install an iron fence around the pool. They're oblivious to our presence.

After laughing about our travel stresses and enjoying a local beer, Craig, the kids, and I walked back to our two-hundred-year-old charming French Château. Opening the door, we notice a nasty oil smell emanating from the basement—perhaps a few caseloads of Febreze will take care of the odor.

However, first things first, tomorrow we have to locate the grocery store, I'll think about the odor another day.

• • •

Madame Baroness (château owner) phones at 8:30 A.M. the following morning with a brisk reminder, "Children in wet bathing costumes are not to sit on the furniture." Still asleep due to jetlag, her request seems completely inane. She wakes us up for this? Apparently, we looked like simpletons when we toured the house. The blame goes entirely to my sister, who smiled like Cheshire cat during our first meeting with the Baroness. We Americans exude a natural friendliness that thus far is wasted in our small neighborhood. (Maybe that will change when our neighbors get to know us.) Still, I'm eager to question the crone about the caretaker's husband who wanders in and out of the house as if he owns the place, however Craig hangs up the phone in a jet-lagged blur. Yesterday the caretaker's grandchildren happily frolicked in our pool, the pool attached to the property that WE rented. I wonder if they're going to pay a pool fee.

The promised re-wiring of the office isn't complete or even started, which poses a large problem. Our original intent before we moved here was to manage our commercial real-estate business from France by Internet and phone. I guess the promise of the fully equipped office was lost in translation or ignored. Thus far, we've blown out two transformers, hastily purchased from the nearby village of Sur Du Lac. Fire and smoke erupt from the small office computer while Craig makes his own sort of smoke with his foul language. This necessitates a trip to the Carrefour, the French equivalent of Wal-Mart, only four times larger.

Negotiating the Neighborhood

Carrefour is hands down the worst shopping experience of my life. Not only does it require an hour-long drive, but it's very difficult to find. We mistakenly drove on the back roads instead of the *autoroute*; the back roads were very skinny, as are the Carrefour store aisles. Perhaps this accounts for all of the dented store carts and large misshapen trucks on the road.

Lacking a navigation system in our minivan, we drove by the store three times. I don't know how we missed it because the parking lot was massive, leaving the warehouse-sized store a mere speck in the distance. The gigantic shopping carts were locked together with a chain and with no directions on how to release them. Rick, Shannon, Craig, and I stood in puzzlement and fiddled with the chain for twenty minutes. We dug about in our pockets and tried a various assortment of coins to no avail. A passing Englishman took pity on us and instructed us how to properly release the shopping cart from its prison. Four college-educated adults couldn't recognize that the coin-sized slot needed a special coin to release the cart. We hiked the long distance to Carrefour from our remote spot in the parking lot to procure the unique coin to release the cart, however, we weren't discouraged—it was all part of the adventure.

Carrefour is like a circus. Locals pushing, shoving; it's Costco on steroids. Crashing of rickety-wheeled carts without so much as an *excusez-moi,* as customers race up and down the aisles like autos at the Monte Carlo Grand Prix. What an adventure, and the attire . . . skin-tight clothing, regardless of body type, and every shade of henna-colored hair known to hairdressers. Bozo the Clown would have felt right at home in this warehouse for the insane.

The store is the size of Costco, however the merchandise doesn't remotely resemble the giant multi-packaged items available at the giant warehouse. We searched for a multi-pack potato chip bag for the kids' lunches only to find single measly twelve-ounce bags at an astronomical price. The small outdoor fruit market in our hometown offered better quality produce than Carrefour and better service. I hoped to see some sort of helper in the store and figured that hand signals would most likely have to suffice as my mode of communication. As I scoured the hair product aisles, I realized I didn't know the word for curling iron. Naturally, I looked for someone with enviable hair; compliments are obvious in any language. Once I located a hair-worthy French person, I used my pigeon-French and fluffed my unkept hair until she either, ran out of patience with me or understood my mimes. *J'ai les cheveux comme la votre?* or I have hair like yours? She smiled and said very slowly, *Suivez-moi,* (follow me) and walked away while gesturing for me to follow her. I thanked her profusely as she and her friend patiently explained through hand signals exactly which hair utensil I should use. Feeling ebullient from this small victory, I located Craig in the wiring department. He located yet a third transformer and we shoved our overloaded cart to the checkout counter. Our shopping experience in Carrefour lasted approximately two hours. We experienced no trouble checking out because Craig bagged our purchases while I removed them from the cart. As we hiked back to the car in the expansive parking lot, we decided Carrefour would be relegated as a "destination spot" for visitors who overstayed their welcome.

We are quickly learning that French portions, whether it is packaging in a warehouse store like Carrefour or restaurant serving sized are quite small as compared to the United States. This is actually a welcome change coming from the land of super-size fries.

Shannon and Rick are waiting at the car in a near panic, their youngest, Kevin, is ready for a nap, as evidenced by his acrobatic-like contortions in his mother's arms. We've all had enough for one day and slowly navigate our way back to Grasse.

The following morning all of us are up early due to continuing jet lag and decide to walk to the nearest town. It is a lovely day to explore our neighborhood and the nearby towns of Châteauneuf de Grasse and Sur Du Lac. In Sur Du Lac, the five of us sit at the sidewalk café for an hour and people-watch, most amusing. The French have a habit of parking their autos wherever they want, which can create some disturbance, if, the spot is in the middle of the road. Generally, there's a lot of shouting and arm waving back and forth when the driver vacates the vehicle for a length of time and others want to get around the car. Maryann actually warned us to "never leave your cars on the road" (meaning park them in your driveway rather than the side street) because passing overloaded trucks commonly hit cars parked on the side of the road.

Our waiter at the small café is very kind. Much to my children's chagrin, I try my caveman French on him and he replies in kind. He understands my French because he smiles at me in a very friendly way as if expecting me to laugh. He says, "I make joke." Perhaps by the end of ten months, I will comprehend French jokes. I don't know.

After our excursion in Sur du Lac, we walked over to Shannon and Rick's for dinner and discovered that they, too, had a few glitches in their home. For some reason this makes me rather pleased, which I know will result in bad karma. As we climbed over the front entry gate, we assured Rick it posed no problem, although Rick is rather miffed at his inability to operate the gate.

Before I climbed over the gate, I had a word with the gate repairman. Perhaps he knew someone who could fix the fouled up antiquated wiring in our home or at least recommend someone. *"Travail pour mon ordinateur?"* On the other side of the fence, Shannon was bent over in hysterics as Monsieur Gate-fixer gave me a perplexed look. I later discovered my mistake, apparently translated as "Can you get a job for my computer?" Naturally, I assumed the words "job" and "work" are the same. I wanted to say, "You know someone who works on computers?" A simple enough mistake.

The comings and goings of the "punch list" laborers are driving Rick and Shannon mad; the house wasn't quite finished. They told us the French work on "French time." I'm not quite sure what that is yet.

After our visit with Rick and Shannon we headed off to the local grocery store in the nearby town of Opio; Le Champion. We nicknamed the store "The Mushroom" because of the similar French spelling of the word mushroom, *champignon.*

After our shopping disaster at Carrefour we feared another semi-large grocery, but decided to take the bull by the horns. Not everything can be purchased in the appealing outdoor markets that line the town streets each morning.

During our shopping (shopping by pictures), several things occurred when we tried to check out at the register. First, the grocery clerk tossed our carefully bagged fruit back down the conveyer belt accompanied by angry gestures. A kind person behind me said, "Zee vegetables must be weighed before you check-out." It's obvious that we're foreigners posing as locals, sympathetic looks are exchanged among the others waiting in line. They've obviously witnessed inept shoppers before. However, the fruit and vegetable weighing procedure isn't as easy as it sounds. Fortunately, pictures of fruit and vegetables are prominently displayed above the scale in the produce aisle for the intellectually challenged. Sadly, our red onions don't make the cut because we couldn't ascertain a price for them. I didn't dare ask the clerk for help, she seemed to be super-glued to her swivel stool. The line of six people waited while the scowling clerk shouted and waved her hands at us as we scurried back and forth to the produce section. Finally, with our lettuce and oranges correctly bagged and marked with the appropriate price, we unloaded the remainder of our groceries on the quickly moving conveyer belt.

Problems ensued when I realized that we were also expected to bag our groceries in the flimsy plastic bags provided. As I ran from one side of the counter to the other to bag the groceries, and then put them in the cart I couldn't help but resent the cashier staring at me from her lofty position on her swivel stool, but no more than I resented Craig who suddenly disappeared into thin air as I was about to have a nervous breakdown. Bagging food is surprisingly stressful. I just don't have the "fast twitch" muscles required for this common chore. No wonder the French are so thin, they must all have high metabolisms and "fast twitch" muscles which enable them to load up their bags in superhero quick fashion.

I much prefer to shop in the village stalls where fresh vegetables, meat, and bread markets are available. They at least weigh and bag your produce; however I once again crossed the French line even in this simple task. I naturally picked up my pears to test them with a slight squeeze. The clerk quickly grabbed my piece of fruit and let me know directly that only he can pick up the fruit. I won't make that mistake again.

Query: "Why do some French citizens wear scowls in place of a smile?" I noticed this as I shopped from day to day. I tried to strike up a limited conversation with my toothy smile as I stopped at the same markets day after day. No smiles ensued from my French neighbors. Only later do I discover the French must truly "know" a person or patron before engaging in conversation. I'm an outsider—for now.

New Kids on the Block and the Autoroute

*T*he *payage* (toll booth) on the *Autoroute* proves that we are ducks out of water. After backing up our mini-van several times because we are in the incorrect line for the *payage*, we finally deduce how to read the well-placed signs. There's a "pass" lane, a "correct change" lane and an "everything else" lane. We're no longer backing out of the incorrect lanes with all other drivers honking at us. It's a good thing we have sort of figured out the *Autoroute* because tomorrow we must navigate our way to the International School of Nice for the kids' first day of school.

The drive into Nice takes approximately an hour, one-way. This is why we wanted to live close to a school, we most likely would have picked out homes closer to Nice had we not expected the kids to start at the Mougins School, which is far closer to our homes.

The day starts nicely, if you disregard the scraping of the brand-new, leased minivan along a rock wall. Actually, Craig scraped the rear tire along a rock wall, backing up a steep road just outside our driveway gate. No damage to speak of (damage is relative, only the really big dents count.) Craig and I delivered the children to school in Nice without any other incidents. On the way home on a winding, narrow, single-lane road, we were passed by some whacked-out, teenage punk in a wussy little Subaru. Craig's manhood was challenged, he responded with a quick downshift of the Renault-Espace (the "Ferrari of mini-vans"), and the chase was on. I thought he was driving reck-lessly, but the truth of the matter is, the Espace is a true thoroughbred. We took the corners on two wheels without any noticeable loss of control. We passed concrete trucks on a hill in a jiffy and we caught up with Subaru (at the next stoplight.) I didn't understand the point, but Craig tells me a man needs to "up his game" when challenged.

As we wait at the securely-gated school and chat with other new parents, Conner runs out the entrance in a dither, "Mom, this is Josh, can he come home with us today?" Conner is enchanted with school, however he says his science teacher is scary, "The teacher has jars of dead floating frogs, and skulls sitting around the classroom, I think our teacher is a wizard or some-thing." Leslie and Austin remain jet-lagged; they don't have Conner's energy level. I myself am only thinking of an alternate method for transporting the kids to school. This driving back and forth could seriously interrupt my time to explore the countryside while the kids are in school.

With some trepidation, we put all of the kids on the bus today; this includes Rick and Shannon's four- and six-year-olds. Shannon feels a bit guilty as little four-year-old Seanie has his forlorn face pressed against the bus window; hopefully, his older cousins will look after him. The bus stop is in a location that we aren't familiar with, and for some reason Craig decided to take a "short cut" to it. Of course, we haven't lived here long enough to know ANY short cuts. I'm reminded of the days of Craig's leading me down goat-trails and shale cliffs while dirt bike riding.

On our "shortcut" we barely avoided a steep drop off in the minivan and then careened around three hairpin curves, all of this on a one-way road . . . going the wrong way. Of course, we lost Rick and Shannon who followed us to the new bus stop. I can just imagine Rick and Shannon's choice words to each other regarding Craig. Craig is clueless sometimes. I chatted with Shannon once we arrived at the bus stop and asked her if she wanted to go to "The Mushroom" with me. She declined, perhaps still smarting from being ditched by Craig. Craig and I ventured forth to "The Mushroom" to buy a cake mix for Leslie's upcoming birthday.

Shopping and Cooking by Pictures

Grocery shopping takes at least one hour because we have trouble deciphering labels. I can't read the French labels; therefore we're reduced to shopping by pictures until I perfect my ability to read French. I discovered an "English" food section in the store, but there's a difference between "English" and "American" food. Rows of Marmite and biscuits, such as Burtons Jammie Dodgers, (two biscuits with raspberry jam in the middle) line the shelf. I myself am not partial to Marmite, which resembles some sort of crude oil in a squatty jar. Marmite is a dark brown, spreadable yeast derivative and, I'm told, "very salty." However, since Americans are in the minority in the ex-pat community, it makes perfect sense to stock mostly English food in this small section of the store. We're overjoyed to see such delights as Skippy peanut butter, enchilada mix, and pancake mix, although I notice that there isn't a single box of Kraft Macaroni and Cheese, the kids will exist on these staples until we figure out how to cook in our antiquated kitchen. I loitered in the store a bit hoping to hear some English voices; perhaps someone will know which box or can contains some frosting for my cake mix.

We successfully bagged our groceries in the rapid-fire manner the clerk expected and leave very pleased with ourselves.

After completing our shopping expedition to "The Mushroom," we drive into town to buy some baguettes from the *boulangerie*. Craig is beside himself with the bargain values of the fresh, long crusty tubes of bread. He buys ten baguettes for tonight's dinner; there are five of us. I enjoy shopping in the small stalls because I can practice my French with the locals. I overheard the *boucherie* (meat store) proprietor whisper to his assistant, "She can understand but she can't speak." Perhaps a backhanded compliment . . . I waved goodbye to Monsieur, and Craig shouted a hearty "Mercy, mercy." I make a mental note to shop without Craig until he can at least say, *"Merci"* properly.

Later that evening, as I unwrap the butcher-papered chicken quaintly tied with string, I nearly faint with dismay. *Monsieur Poulet* still sports numerous feathers and both of his feet. Thinking back on our transaction, I crowed out my order, *"Je veux le poulet."* Translated as "Me want chicken." He then smiled (one of the few vendors who shows his teeth) and quickly wrapped up the chicken. I paid him no mind because the hogs hanging in the breezeway proved an unappetizing distraction. In hindsight, I now realize he must have responded; "Do you prefer your chicken with feet?" My language skills being limited, I missed this part of the conversation. (And the hog distracted me.) So I closed my eyes and sawed off his feet, fully expecting to hear a squawk. I now have two clawed feet resting peacefully on the counter. What to do with the feet? Is it acceptable to throw appendages in the garbage? I toss them in the garbage and resolve to take the garbage to the curb myself. Now I must tackle my antiquated oven.

The dinosaur oven presents a few problems, the temperature dial is a mystery and requires a bit of guesswork. I located an old pan pre-seasoned with leftover chickens from days gone by, and wonder if the past *poulet* retained their feet while roasting? Hopefully, I'll regain my appetite after the footless chicken is cooked. I don't know.

Today is Leslie's birthday and I'm concerned. Naturally, Leslie expects a cake on her birthday. How will I cook the cake with my antiquated stove when I have yet to figure out the temperature dial? The chicken from last night's dinner was reduced to cinders because I couldn't figure out the oven thermometer.

Loud noises emanate from the dark hole of the kitchen. Craig finds me rattling around in drawers and cursing anything within shouting distance. I can't find the weights needed to make the blasted cake; cups and teaspoons are not recognized in baking language here. In Europe, dry ingredients are measured by weight. A thorough scouring of the kitchen produces no scale. As far as I'm concerned, cooking requires a masters degree in math. Grams, kilos measuring by metric unit, and the oven temperature is in Celsius. Despite the conversions necessary, I managed to put the cake together and shoved it into my dilapidated oven.

My tired old oven produced a chocolate Mount Fuji, I'm sure my measurements are near correct so it must be the fault of the oven. I deeply regret not making the cake in a sheet pan. In order to rectify my mistake, I paste the runny frosting/pudding on the cake. The results are worse than I expect, and even I recognize my cake won't pass muster at school or at home.

Later that night, we feasted on Mt. Fuji after a rousing Happy Birthday chorus. Cups (or is it weights of milk) are required to digest the dry tinder log posing as a cake. Leslie thanks me profusely for my attempt at baking a cake for her. "It only looks bad, Mama, it didn't taste bad." Bless her.

The Wind That Blows— Le Mistral

Sleep eluded us last night because the mistral visited in the middle of the night. The mistral is a fierce cold wind that blows off the Alps at certain times of the year. I remember the mistrals very clearly from long ago when I lived as a student in Avignon for three months. Unfortunately, I lacked gloves and hat for the long hike to school in the cold biting wind.

Our fine, old eighteenth-century home (with the seventeenth-century electric wiring) holds up to the high winds, but the heavy wooden storm shutters we carefully secured banged all night. The front door handle malfunctioned (fell off) as we locked up for the evening. Of course, during the big wind the downstairs front door blew open in the middle of the night. We now have a screwdriver placed in the lock in order to keep the door shut. Craig—not bothered by the winds sits up late mapping out our first bike ride for tomorrow.

The French Ride Bikes— Don't They?

The bike ride didn't go according to plan.

Today, we toured the nearby French hospital in Grasse, and I tried to speak at length to some very nice French doctors and six *gendarmes* (policemen.) Actually, I garbled my caveman French with the doctors and in my distress waved my hands about with the policeman. It all started innocently enough.

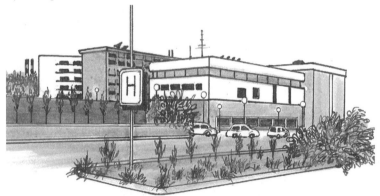

Enthusiastic to ride our new bikes, Craig planned our ride on the back roads; naturally we wanted to avoid traffic on our first bike ride. At first, we cycle by scenic pastures and old men smoking cigarillos as they stroll along the country roads. The passing cars give us plenty of room, the bikers have complete right of way here. No one honks at bikers; they're treated with respect in this country. This is the home of the Tour de France.

We approached a roundabout, the very sensible French equivalent of an American stoplight. It takes a bit of nerve to sprint into the roundabout circle as the cars literally race around the loop like some miniature version of the Grand Prix. I feel a bit vulnerable merging with the cars but there are no bike paths, and bikes follow the same rules as the cars. Naturally, I insist that Craig dart out into the traffic circle first.

The next thing I see is Craig's body flying through the air, arms and legs akimbo. An elderly French driver crossed lanes right in front of him, because she wanted to exit from the roundabout. Craig lands on his butt, his back, and then his head. I scream, *"Il est moi, il est moi,"* which means, "It is me, it is me," I meant to yell *"Aidez- moi, aidez- moi."* The latter translates to "Help me! Help me!" Under duress, my French comes out completely muddled and none of the good French Samaritans who have stopped to help understand a word I'm saying. A British ex-pat stops to help me; she translates for the police officers and the ambulance personnel who arrive rapidly to the scene of the accident.

For some reason, the police officer draws a chalk mark around my prostrate husband before putting him in the ambulance. I silently wonder (Would they think I'm a raving lunatic if I asked in my one-syllable language?) if they plan to use the scene of the accident for some type of reality show. Either way, the finality of the chalk mark isn't good for me. Why don't they pick my poor spouse up and carry him to the ambulance? Determined to help my husband (who, of course, says he is fine), I firmly speak my caveman lingo and throw in a few hand signals for good effect, but the officers just shake their heads sadly.

The woman who hit my husband is visibly distraught. As Craig slowly rises from his chalk marked position, the first thing he does is comfort the old gal. My still-reeling spouse gently puts an arm around the shaking women, trying to show her that he isn't seriously injured. She draws away with no eye contact. According to French custom, it's a national disgrace to run over a bicyclist. She walks with her head down toward the beckoning gendarme.

As the gendarme valiantly tries to explain to me (in English) what needs to be done before leaving the scene, Craig is climbing into the ambulance. "Shawn, you stay here and find someplace safe to store the bikes." So, not only do I have to find a safe place for the bikes, but then I must find my way to the hospital instead of riding in the ambulance as any good spouse would do.

Since I see that Craig doesn't seem to be seriously injured, I get mad at the whole situation. What am I supposed to do with the bikes? How am I supposed to dictate a police report when I can barely speak the language? How do I get to the hospital? The policemen take pity on me and hand me a business card. We're supposed to report to the police station tomorrow or as soon as possible, to complete the police report. I heave a sigh of relief and then contemplate where I'm going to store the bikes. As the policemen wait, I run across the street to the *poulet roti* (roasted chicken) shack. The owner witnessed the accident and thoughtfully agrees to take care of the bikes.

The mostly silent ride to the hospital only takes about ten minutes; I carefully noted the location of the hospital in case of future disasters. Luckily, the woman at the front desk says "can I help you?" in English and we quickly locate Craig holding court in a private room. Craig immediately asks; "Did you find a place for the bikes?" Men . . . I would have liked to talk about my obvious distress at watching him ride away in the ambulance or ME dealing with the policemen.

The French have National Health Care regardless of citizenship status. Craig received a thorough exam, his cracked helmet being enough proof of a possible head injury. After a clear MRI, the doctor thoughtfully, yet sternly, explains to Craig that he must learn the French language while living here in France. For some reason, this makes me absurdly happy, as he had dismissed my ideas of studying the language before we arrived in France, not that my previous studying helped me this morning in my efforts to communicate my distress.

The hospital receptionist called a cab for us, a huge relief because I had no idea how to use the phone booth and we didn't have a cell phone. The phone booth needed some sort of card to operate it and I didn't know where to get a card. Mundane tasks that require no thought in the United States take on immense proportions overseas. On the way home I showed Craig the location of the bikes at *poulet roti*, relief is evident on his face. The darn bikes are worth a fortune. Luckily, Craig's bike received only a few dings, proof of his manly escape from the speeding car.

The World Changes

L ife in southern France is just taking on a semblance of normality when all Hell breaks loose in the United States. The attack on the Twin Towers in New York happens. No words describe the helplessness we experience for the people (our people) of the United States. While waiting in the Nice airport for Shannon's nanny, Crystal, and Licky, their dog, a German fellow approached us to impart the news.

The German visitor recognized our American accents and asked what Shannon and I thought of the news. We both look at him with complete incomprehension, thinking his sense of humor is morbid at best. Stunned and shaken, we greet Crystal and quickly rush to the car and turn on the local English radio station. After departing from the plane, Crystal is equally surprised. The first plane hit the World Trade Center only two hours before she arrived, so, she was actually in the air when the devastation occurred.

Crystal didn't get much of a reception because we all rushed over to Rick and Shannon's home (we have no English-speaking channels,) where we watched CNN trying to get an idea of what's happening in the United States.

Reading the International News Tribune and the USA Today newspapers the following day, each details vivid descriptions of the destruction caused by the two planes.

We begin to hear from our friends in the United States and the news is frightening, at best:

•••

To: Craig and Shawn

It is unbelievable what is happening in New York and on the East Coast right now. Here, they have evacuated the Columbia Tower and the Space Needle, and the ferries are not allowing cars. All airports are closed. Since I'm still on staff at Swedish Hospital, I may be called in for a Code Delta Alert.

•••

To: Craig and Shawn

I have no doubt that you have heard about the horrible happenings here on the East Coast. You must be happy to be in another country. I'm curious to know reactions abroad.

Believe it or not, we are all very much affected here in Seattle so far away from the actual attacks, but it all hits so close to the heart. It is so strange to see no planes flying in and out of Sea-Tac from our viewpoint. Also hearing lots of military planes flying around in the middle of the night.

Seattle basically shut down yesterday; everyone is staying home for fear of going into any public place where they might be vulnerable. Most of the bad news is still yet to come—we're hearing they've only found seven survivors so far at the World Trade Center.

Anyway, sorry to be so grim, but thought you might like a personal update.

•••

To: Craig and Shawn

Crazy week here in the USA, as I'm now sure you know. All of us are still reeling from the events that unfolded before our eyes in NYC and in DC on Tuesday.

•••

To: Craig and Shawn

The country is very emotional here with a Bush prayer meeting today and TV news covering every detail of everything on a 24-7 basis. Eighty-three percent of the public polled says U.S. should hammer the bad guys, but 7% say we shouldn't, and 8% don't know. Don't know NBC News was knocked off the air just now due to NYC power failure and Congress appropriated $40 billion for repairs and war costs with a resolution to Bush that he is authorized to punish the perpetrators and to take steps to prevent further similar events. Pretty broad authority. The news is filled with reports that prove quickly to be false, so nobody knows much except that they sure knocked the Hell out of NYC. The bond markets are reasonably stable except for having risen dramatically due to anticipated Fed cut rates. Stock markets did not open today as had been announced.

No sporting events except high school and the annual Police "Bacon Bowl," which will probably sell out the Tacoma Dome. An email went around the nation today calling for a national vigil at 1900 ET where everyone was to come out on his or her lawn and hold a candle signifying solidarity. Didn't go over well here, as it is still broad daylight, thus candles are not too effective. The news is full of reports of American pressure on Pakistan to permit over flights and possibly stationing of troops and use of airfields and facilities. The country seems like somebody pushed the "hold" button at the moment, but I don't think it's going to remain that way very long.

∾ Part III ∾

Treading Water

Fort Knox—
Our New Home

Maryann (our real estate agent) is finalizing some legal papers for Rick and Shannon at their house. Naturally she asks us how things are going. Craig and I exchanged the "should we tell her" look. Maryann sees the look and exclaims, "What, is there something wrong?" We relate the sad saga of the Baroness's grandchildren loudly playing in the pool at all hours, and of the caretaker's husband traipsing in and out of the basement as if he owned the place, and of course the noxious odor emanating from the basement. The multitudes of destroyed computer transformers we buy because of the ragged old wiring that still isn't replaced as promised. Maryann is appalled, furious actually, and chastises us for not calling her sooner. Relief is evident in our faces as Maryann vows to locate us a different place and get our deposit returned.

The sainted Maryann searches high and low and locates an updated house in the same neighborhood. She reveals that the Norwegian couple are friends of hers and don't usually rent their home, however the couple plan to be away for a year and are willing to show us their home. I'm a bit dubious because this scenario sounds exactly like the one from our last landlord. Our antiquated chateau is lovely to look at but doesn't function as we expected. No tears will be shed when and if we leave our dilapidated manse.

Maryann's friends have no children and our kids must pass muster before the owners will rent to us. They are art collectors and their house isn't "child-proof." We are fairly certain the kids can hold it together for an hour or so and frankly the kids are ready to move from the old manse.

On our way to the new rental, Craig and I managed to get lost five times. It is less than three miles away. There's minimal yelling and cursing from either of us, getting lost is routine in France. The kids remained quiet in the back of the car although we're a bit worried our annoying kids might act up with their usual bickering and fighting. As a precaution to possible rambunctious behavior, we bribe the children with a McDonald's meal, an unpleasant reminder of our previous life.

Craig and I finally located the gated driveway to our possible new home. The owners buzz us in from the speakerphone attached to the gatepost. As Craig and I climb the formidable driveway in our minivan (three hairpin turns on a gravel road,) we see the newly constructed "old home." Bright blue shutters give the windows an old world charm and the whitewashed stucco looks as if it has been there for centuries. In contrast to the old world look—the parking pad of the driveway is paved and immense steel rolldown garage doors make a formidable basement entry. Exiting the car, we search for the front door and locate it on the other side of the house.

Björn, a giant of a man, opens the front door and booms a loud hello in a Norwegian accent. His petite blond wife, Petrina, warmly greets us in French although she is also Norwegian. It's the second home of a Norwegian couple, and they've no plans for visiting in the coming year. Looking out the kitchen window at the pastoral Grasse valley, I realize we'll be quite isolated; mistral winds and rains could trap us for days at a time.

The interiors are furnished with unique artwork. Petrina modestly admits to being an artist and by the variety of her work, she seems to be a very good one. Two giant Greek pillars stand between the kitchen and the kitchen table, giving me pause. I unobtrusively tap one to measure the steadiness of the column. I can just see the kids knocking one over to shatter in a million pieces on the tiled floor. Another interesting décor feature is Björn's collection of old World War II airplane wing replicas, complete with worn painted bathing beauties and bullet holes. Craig is enamored with these old relics as well as the framed yellowed newspaper clippings of Hitler's demise. The kitchen contains commercial equipment for cooking, and a butler's pantry complete with a Starbucks-sized espresso machine. This is obviously the home of a childless couple, no rumpled carpets, stained couches, or a game room. The Stenums entertain a lot as evidenced by the list of favorite chefs, caterers, and florists that Petrina uses when in town.

Thoroughly updated on the inside yet cozy and comfortable, the three-storied home is surrounded by acres of olive groves and boasts an Olympic-sized swimming pool with a view of the Mediterranean. A quaint laundry line strung between two olive trees is visible outside the pantry window. Petrina says they never use the dryer because the wind-blown sheets smell much better.

Because the house sits atop a very high hill, the Stenums are equipped for storms with a Carrefour supply of candles and long heavy metal flashlights in each room. The flashlights are police issue, doubling as head bashers. Björn points out the red mobile panic buttons in each and every room. Why all the security precautions? Who is this guy and who does he work for? I immediately deduced the Norwegian couple must be spies. Why the need for all of the safety measures and why are they leaving the country for a whole year? Whatever the reason, I pray we make a good impression on our first visit.

Perhaps reading my thoughts, (about the panic button, not the spy theory) Petrina explained petty crime is rampant in France, and especially on the Riviera, a popular tourist spot. Several years earlier Björn and Petrina experienced a theft while sunning outside by the pool, hence the heavy-duty alarm system. The thief crept in and out of the house without the owners knowing until they witnessed him running up the back hillside from the house. The panic buttons aren't the only deterrent in and around our house.

A steel box encloses the outside phone wiring for our home as a precaution for intruders cutting the wires. There's a secure gate from the patio to the pool and a secure gate at the end of our very long, dirt, and pot-holed driveway. Our bedroom is on the top floor of the house, it doubles as a "panic room," and both doors that lead to the room are solid steel. The panic room is a final security measure for the home occupants if robbers breach the inside of the home. Both Craig and I are astounded at this amount of security. What if we lock ourselves out of the burglar-proof renovated house or worse yet, press the panic button when Leslie gets up to go to the loo? At the time, we thought the extent of security precautions to be overkill.

Despite the intimidating security system, Craig and I are relieved that the owners like our kids and us and decide to rent to us, despite our obvious lack of understanding of the mechanics of the high-tech house. The kids are overjoyed because they get to go to McDonald's.

• • •

Craig's Observations

This afternoon, Shawn and I toured a home owned by a Norwegian couple. They completely renovated the old home, retaining the charm on the exterior but changing the interior to reflect their Twenty-first century techno tastes. The garage even has a "quick lube" setup, if I need a second career. We would like to rent a different home from the one we are in, one with clothes dryer, functioning electrical wiring, and a microwave. Is this too much to ask for a year sabbatical in France? We found out tonight that we can move on September 15, provided we work out an exit with the owner of the shack we are presently leasing.

The Baroness seems relieved that we want out of the lease, however even after Maryann points out the lack of proper wiring for our computers and the trespassing grandchildren, the Baroness won't return our last month rent which we left on deposit.

• • •

Post 9/11

We've had an interesting couple of weeks since the attacks of September 11. I can't describe the feeling of watching CNN, Fox, and MSNBC from France while all Hell is breaking loose at home.

We feel safe here, for now. Kids are doing well in school, but French is a struggle for the boys. Leslie and I went shopping yesterday, "retail therapy." It was the first time we ventured out of one of the small villages and to an actual mall. The only real difference we noted was the lack of any place to sit in the mall corridors. The French don't do fast food. A meal is an occasion to relax, enjoy the food, and engage in stimulating conversation. Leslie and I left the mall hungry.

On September 16, we hosted a party for all the American families we've met through the International School of Nice. It was great to be together, to celebrate being Americans, to eat BBQ hamburgers and hot dogs, potato chips, baked beans, Toll House cookies, Coca-Cola, and Corona Beer (Mexico is close enough). You have no idea how hard it is to find hotdog and hamburger buns in France. One of the hot topics of discussion other than the tragic news of 9/11, was the food cravings we are all experiencing. Surprisingly, you can't find Cheese Whiz or Velveeta in French grocery stores. The top four products missed most by the kids were Jif Peanut Butter, French's Yellow Mustard, Grape Nuts cereal, and of course, Kraft Macaroni and Cheese. One of the husbands flew in from Chicago on the afternoon of the party and brought us a jar of Jif Peanut Butter, he's a friend for life.

Everyone shares their overseas 9/11 stories and news from friends back home. Good portions of the Americans here hail from New York and most have lost someone they know. The group of us mutually decides to:

1. Register with the United States Embassy here in France in the remote possibility that things turn sour here.

2. Acquire new license plates. We all have leased cars with RED license plates as opposed to the local non-red French license plates.

3. Contact friends in nearby European countries in case we need to suddenly leave France and can't make it to the United States.

Looking back, these plans seem extreme, but at the time we had no idea how 9/11 would affect the world as a whole. Even here in France; none of us feels safe from harm, more like "sitting ducks" as Americans with telltale red license plates.

French Time = Come Back Tomorrow

L ast week, we decided to finally get mobile phones from a French-based carrier to stay in contact with our many new friends, to allow the children's teachers to call us during the school day if necessary, and to call the police if we have more bad luck on the bikes. We visit one store, hoping someone can speak English and are rewarded with a nice young man who understands every single word (if we speak slowwwwwly.) We ordered two "prepaid" phones rather than "subscription" phones. The prepaid phones must be charged with a bucket of minutes periodically, and you must be fluent in French to accomplish this.

The nice young salesman apparently understood the 5th, 10th, and 15th words of our request and offered to charge our phones with 100 minutes each upon payment of an outrageous sum equal to fifty cents/minute. Unfortunately, he's unable to make contact with the carrier and tells us "No minutes for you, come back tomorrow." The phrase: "No (insert item) for you, come back later to the; roasted chicken store; the baguette store; the bank; and the Hospital ER is commonly used here in France . . . at least with us. Life in France is at a slower pace than what we're used to.

The next day, we come back promptly at 8 a.m., when the phone store opens. The nice man tries again in vain to charge our phones with minutes. "No minutes for you, come back tomorrow" is again the mantra. Maybe we're also supposed to buy a TV, stereo, or satellite dish before he will make the phones functional. I'm just not sure. He has a for sale sign on his beat-up car in the parking lot; maybe we need to make an offer. We decided that we don't want another electronic device in Maison Fort Knox and we don't need a second car, so we wave good-bye and tell him we will be back tomorrow. On the third day, we meet with success. We have had "charged" phones for four days now and have a total of zero calls and zero messages. We are so popular.

Driving Like a Frenchman

Today and every day, I drive my darling minivan. I'm not normally a minivan sort of person, images of housewives in curlers dance in my head. There's no such thing as a Chevy Suburban here and the gas would be prohibitive, so the minivan is the next best thing. I now know to honk my horn when I veer around a corner on a steep single-track road. My minivan has experienced close contact with rock walls, flying onions, and the ever-present potholes.

I nearly hit a dog that had the nerve to be on the single-track road; instead I flew over a giant rock and careened into some bushes on the side of the road. Shannon happened to be in the car and she let out quite a yelp, entirely unnecessary. She said I would be the premature death of her. She tends to exaggerate when she's afraid. We merely scraped some paint off the passenger side of the car, and put a small dent on the side. However, the car is so dirty that it's likely that no one will notice.

• • •

Craig's Observations on Shawn's Driving

Shannon and Shawn drove the Renault Espace (the Ferrari of minivans) to pick-up the children from school this afternoon. Upon their return, I noticed a dent in the hood, and scratched paint. I calmly asked them at the dinner table, what could have caused such damage? Their answer was nothing short of incredible. According to their sworn testimony, they were following (at a safe distance) a large open truck filled with onions when two large onions fell off, bounced off the roadway and onto the hood of our Ferrari of minivans. I was skeptical, knowing the responsive steering, acceleration, and braking capabilities of our vehicle.

I followed up with the clincher: How could an onion dent AND SCRATCH the hood? They were very calm in their response, obviously rehearsed all the way home from school, "The onions picked up some gravel when they bounced off the roadway." It is tough to catch any pair of sisters in a lie. I will have to try harder. I pursued another tack of questioning to see if they would break, "Onions falling off a truck sounds close to the old fable of immigrants falling off the turnip truck." Not a blink of an eye, not a twitch, nothing. They sat there stone-faced, nodding. I have hit a dead end, for now, but maybe when we open the bottles of champagne this weekend to formally celebrate our arrival in France something will slip out. We'll see.

• • •

"Monte"

This weekend we visited Monaco. San Remo, Italy is our first stop as Shannon says there's a marvelous restaurant somewhere in the town. San Remo is past Monaco, but Shannon insists that the restaurant is just over the next hill. The countryside is littered with long clear plastic greenhouses containing lush tomatoes in their humid interiors, but not the elusive restaurant.

Having been on the road for two hours, everyone in the car is crabby and Rick is ready to eat his arm. (Rick has low blood sugar.) Things deteriorate even more because Shannon is navigating. Shannon refuses to concede that we are lost. Craig and I listen to their curt words from the back seat; we attempt to give helpful suggestions but are tersely rebuffed. I suggest perhaps Rick isn't at his best due to his low blood sugar. A stiff silence entombs the car; we're still on the road to nowhere. There's a mumbled suggestion by someone to head back to Monaco and Rick leaps at the idea. Somehow we find our way.

The Hermitage Hotel in Monaco is one of the oldest and most renowned hotels in the area; fortunately, all of the plumbing is updated. As usual, there's no shower but there is a bathtub with a handheld shower faucet. This particular method of washing still remains cumbersome, even after being here for nearly a month. Holding the handheld spray faucet while attempting to wash my hair remains a mystery to me. I can only conclude the French must be ambidextrous or unusually agile. I usually spray the entire bathroom and then slip and fall on my butt when I leave the pseudo shower tub.

We shopped around the main part of the small town before dinner, but the prices discouraged any buying, even the deliciously skimpy "smalls" (underwear) the French wear. Later at dinner, Shannon orders everything she hates to eat. When questioned about her unusual ordering habit in the restaurant, she says she is happy with her meal. As her sister, I know she is telling a bit of a fib but I'm unable to get her to admit her ordering peculiarity. She does this quite a bit, and usually ends up eating bread for dinner; at least the bread is "*très bon*" (very good) in France. Shannon then asks to see the dessert menu; she interprets the waiter's response as, "go to the kitchen if you want to see the dessert." I clearly am not the only one who has a problem translating the French dialect, it's different in every city we visit. The waiter will not serve coffee WITH dessert; coffee in France is taken at the end of the meal, AFTER dessert. Another custom we must get used to if we want to appear as locals here.

We went to the Casino after dinner. Because we're in "Monte", we fully expected to see celebrities. Celebrities spotted—zero. Possibly this is because we were too cheap to pay the $5.00 to go in the private rooms—no doubt all of the famous people were in the room with the well-heeled big spenders. I'm pretty sure I saw Claus Van Bulow.

Sleeping in the next morning, an unheard of luxury for parents of young children, we slowly come to the realization that we must drive home and face our lively brood.

At home in Grasse, Rick and Shannon's nanny, Crystal, is exhausted and ready to pull her hair out, "Oh, the kids were great, no problems." We know better, as Conner and Leslie studiously look at the ground. Conner is now spending "quality time" in his bedroom along with his old pal, Leslie. It seems a small scuffle ensued between Conner, Leslie, and Kylie. Inappropriate language (we call it toilet-talk) issued forth from Conner in the heat of battle in front of the other smaller children. Not surprising, although I'm sure the kids have heard most everything on the wretched school bus they ride every day.

If at First You Don't Succeed

After having coffee for longer than necessary (made with our top-grade commercial espresso maker) one morning, we mutually decide it's time to get back on the bikes again. Our expensive road bikes have been gathering dust in the garage ever since Craig's unfortunate run-in with the old lady in the roundabout. This time our planning includes driving about in our minivan and surveying possible routes with the least amount of traffic.

While looking for possible bicycle routes, we toured the mountain town of Gourdon and observed from the comfort of our minivan the lack of traffic. However, this keen observation is tempered by the obvious necessity to climb an extremely steep (3000-foot) "hill." Gourdon boasts an ancient church along with a variety of restaurants carved into the rocks. A perfect midpoint stop for an Orangina (the local fizzy orange drink) and a breather before heading back down the mountain. This, of course, is assuming I make it to the top of the mountain without suffering a heart attack.

Needing moral support and someone a bit more fluent in French (in case of another accident), we invited Rick and Shannon along with us. Rick and Shannon are enthused about our choice of ride and decide to come along for the adventure. We meet in a parking lot at the base of the mountain. Before we scale the mountain on our bikes, two roundabouts loom before us. Naturally, Craig and I are a bit nervous about going through the round-abouts due to our last experience when we attempted to ride with the traffic. Luck is with us this time and we make it through the roundabout without crashing into each other or any other of the box-shaped autos so prevalent in southern France. This is fortunate because Craig still hasn't replaced his dented/cracked helmet, not much use if he dumps his bike yet again. I think he's saving it for posterity.

We start to climb immediately; one doesn't notice steep climbs and gravel-filled shoulders while sitting in a car. My breathing becomes labored within five minutes. I attempt to shout directions at Shannon who's behind me, but I immediately swerved into the oncoming lane (Note to self, don't attempt to ride and talk to the person behind you at the same time.) I give it up as a lost cause. She isn't having much trouble anyway. She catches up to me and I wheeze some incomprehensible advice at her. Being the older sister comes with a "bossy gene."

Despite my labored breathing, I managed to catch a whiff of whatever scent is being concocted at the Gourdon Parfumerie (perfume factory) and make a mental note not to buy whatever it is they're making. As I stop to gulp some water, Shannon rides past; I foolishly believe I will catch up with her. I'm now riding drag; there isn't a soul behind me, just the very steep road with no guardrail on a very high mountain.

Once we've scaled the mountain of Gourdon (me a full ten minutes behind everyone else), a quick tour is in order, but our legs are so wobbly that we opt for a long rest at a nearby café. Naturally, we commend ourselves on our accomplishment, even being so bold as to compare ourselves to riders in the *Tour de France*. "Remember when Lance passed that guy on the incline of Alpe d'Huez?" "Yah, after this ride, I know what he felt like." Hopefully, the patrons in the café lack good English skills because our brag-fest is unfortunately unwarranted. We're pretenders in this country populated with elite bike riders.

Descending is even more harrowing. My hands remain perma-clenched on the brakes as I squeeze every other minute to slow my too-rapid descent down the mountain. I don't dare look behind me as the giant tankers containing the noxious perfume make their way down the mountain. Navigating the pot-holed road is extremely tricky, but I take heart remembering that the French love "the bikers", excepting, of course, for the woman who ran over Craig.

Circus Circus

This afternoon we surprised the kids when we picked them up at the school bus stop. The circus is in town. Circuses are a big deal here, families actually make a living driving from town to town and setting up in an empty lot next to a pasture of wandering horses or goats. There's a traveling circus in nearly every town we go through. Perhaps not quite as showy as the imaginative Cirque du Soleil troupes that tour the United States, but more of a "dog and donkey" show. In this small town extravaganza, a goat demonstrated his talents along with the dog and the donkey. The ten people in our combined families make up the entire audience. The ticket taker is also the ringmaster and the popcorn maker. In the traveling circus trade, the performers must wear many hats or ride the available animals. Everyone has a job.

The donkey and the goat are amusing to watch because they're inured to commands from the boss. The donkey refuses to stand on his teacup platform until he receives his treat. "Pavlov's dog in reverse." When the shaggy goat knocks the circus leader on the behind with his horns, my two-year old nephew, Kevin laughs hysterically. It's funny once, but little Kevin laughed all five times. This particular circus is a family act; the three small children perform strength acts and twirl effortlessly on the trampoline, while the lithe mother skips across a tight rope with nary a wobble. What a life this little family leads.

Four of our six children loved the circus, Austin and Conner pronounced the entire thing "lame." I notice they did appreciate the sugared popcorn the ringmaster served at intermission.

The local newspaper reports Princess Stephanie of Monaco has run away with a circus performer. Shannon and I hoped we might see the princess, at the Goat, Donkey, and Dog circus, sadly she must be in a "higher quality" circus.

We later saw pictures of the Princess in a *Star Magazine*. The gossip rag reports her job is feeding an African elephant, and reportedly, practicing stunts to further her career as a circus performer. She apparently has many talents according to the tabloid.

Antibes

oday we visited Antibes, a harbor town, where we viewed the fishing fleet as well as a few majestic yachts. Antibes is also the home of a giant flea and antique market each weekend. There is a museum in Antibes solely dedicated to Picasso, and the admission is low and well worth the price. Here you can find a history of Picasso and his works, all of which are out in the open, not under Plexiglas protection.

As we wandered around town, we came across a great pottery store that has a perfect tray decorated with olives. Imagining the sweet little tray in my kitchen, I of course want to stop and peruse the store. Shopping with one's family appendages is difficult because Craig and the children dance around impatiently outside each store, thus distracting me from my task at hand. I decided to visit Antibes later while the children are in school and Craig is otherwise occupied.

We stopped for ice cream; the children behaved well for most of the morning, as well as Craig—my most difficult child. The woman next to us has her small fluffy dog in the tiny café. The French bring their dogs every-where; restaurants and cafés aren't off limits. The amorous little dog quite enjoys himself as he humps another patron's leg. Perhaps this is standard in France because the dog-less customer takes no notice. The kids scream with delight, fabulous entertainment for them.

• • •

French Breakfast—
American Style

This morning, I attempted to make an American breakfast with a salt lick posing as a slab of bacon. Maybe it's a piece of ham. I tried to explain to the butcher my idea of American bacon, but I'm not sure he understood my French. Again one guy says in French to the other, "She understands but can't speak well," the ongoing story of my life here in the south of France. After drinking gallons of water to quell the thirst from the salt-lick breakfast, we head out to the racetrack with Shannon and Rick and their three kids.

Some of our ex-pat friends at the International School of Nice wax enthusiastically about this GREAT racetrack on the outskirts of Grasse. Unlike the United States, this adult-sized track has no security personnel, not unusual here in France. The speedy little autos are said to go 100 mph, according to one of the parents. "You gotta see this, you can't believe how fast the cars go!" Craig has a glazed faraway look in his eyes as his testosterone levels rise in accordance with his need for speed.

The male hormone levels creating pre-teen squeaky voices rise to an ear-deafening crescendo in the Ferrari of minivans when we drive to the track that morning.

At the racetrack, Austin squeaks enthusiastically about how fabulous he will be when he actually drives a car; however, the racetrack is closed due to rain. All of the males look longingly at the chained up, souped-up mini race-cars. The racetrack is geared for adult idiots and their offspring. There are no rules posted and no fences, just a track.

In order to appease our disappointed kids, we cajole them into going on a brief "pre-ski" mountain hike. "Let's see how steep these French mountains really are!" We drive to the mountain/hill where there's one ski lift and it's still raining. The little savages are on the verge of an all out rebellion. Food is a great panacea for all ills, and we wisely stop at the first café we see.

Upon entering the café, I politely asked the owner for two tables for ten people, he says, *"Mais non."* (But no.) I respond in my best caveman French, *"Nous buvons,"* (We drink.) He replies, *"d'accord."* (Okay.) Hot chocolate is ordered . . . three times, each time with a different and "new improved" accent, the owner gives me a puzzled look when I add chocolate baguettes to the order. I can see the light go off in his head, *"ahhh, pain au chocolat."* *"Oui,"* I reply. I have no idea what sort of sustenance will arrive after this interlude, but all the same, relief fills me; it's a heavy burden to carry, being the only "fluent" speaker in our family. When I look at my family in triumph because I managed to place this simple order, they studiously ignored me; frankly, I don't know how they'd get by without me.

After our lengthy snack we decided to explore the countryside a bit more before heading home. All the kids moaned in chorus. Trails in France are clearly marked with a red X, very convenient for people who are directionally challenged. Austin groans straight away, "let's just go home." And is immediately ordered back to wait in the car. He can find his way back by the X marks. He happily trots back to the car; he has a good sense of direction. As I watch Craig's undulating hams in front of me, I inquire as to the last time he stepped on the scale. He ignores me.

"My, what an interesting hiking trail," I exclaim as we pass two dilapidated old box-shaped cars and one rusted out refrigerator. Assuming the dump will be just around the corner, and not really enjoying our outdoor excursion, I suggest we head back to the car. Craig readily agrees claiming he knows a "shortcut." "How can you possibly know a shortcut? We've never been here and we have to stay on the path of red X marks or we'll be lost." Not an unreasonable statement on my part. "Just follow me." Sigh.

A half-hour later we continue wandering aimlessly, no red X's in sight. Craig, still positive in his leadership, spies a tall wire fence. A fence that most certainly would stab and bite if one decided to scale said wire fence. Craig says we will scale the fence. "You first, and watch your nether regions," I said. Meanwhile, my son, Conner, thoughtfully walks along the perimeter of the fence and locates a hole, which he shimmies through. Craig and I are still debating who will climb the fence first, when Conner waves from the other side. Problem solved, thanks to Conner who confidently leads us back to the car. "How was the hike?" says Austin. "Dad is fired as hike leader," I say. Conner and Leslie readily agree as we head home from our morning outing.

Le Coupe de Cheveux—
The Haircut

I do admit the language barrier is becoming an increasing problem . . . for Craig. I, on the other hand, am getting along famously, when the French speaker talks SLOWLY. Today, for instance, and after much debate, the kids and I all agreed to brave the hair salon. Unfortunately, the head beautician in the male/female salon is a "fast talker," my pleas of *"lentement, s'il vous plaît,"* (slowly, please) fall on deaf ears and disaster looms on the horizon.

Before driving to the hairdresser for the kid's haircuts, I make a quick phone call to my sister, Shannon, who professes to have mastered the French language. I asked her for the appropriate phrases to use with the hairdresser. "I don't know the word for hedgehog in French," says Shannon. Too bad, the word, hedgehog is a perfect description of Conner's spiky current haircut.

The kids fight on the way to the haircutter about who gets their hair cut first. They're all nervous, I'm not sure if this is about the upcoming trimmings or their lack of faith in my language skills.

We mutually decided that Leslie is first, because her hair is difficult to destroy. I manage to convey my ideas to the beautician, and things go smoothly with Leslie. In the men's section of the salon next door, Austin is about to get his new cut. I'm terribly worried about Austin's hair because he attends his first "teen" party tonight and must look as cool as he believes he is. I greet the barber with a friendly *"bonjour,"* and attempt to give him ideas about Austin's hair. With a combination of pantomime and cobbled together French/English language, I conveyed Austin's hair must be *"bref"* (short or brief) with points on top. When I yanked and pulled on Austin's hair so it stood straight up, the barber nodded that he understood. Of course, Austin is nearly uprooted from his chair, but no matter, I apparently get my point across because Austin's hair looked *"très bon"* (very good) when the barber finished. Conner doesn't have any problems with his hair either. Amazingly, all of the kids are pleased with their haircuts.

I breathe a sigh of relief and attempted to explain to my cranberry-haired beautician my preferred hairstyle. Thinking myself extremely clever, I showed her some likely pictures in a magazine. She ripped the magazine out of my hand and shouted at me in a near hysterical screech; *"Je suis artiste,"* (I'm an artist,) and things go from bad to worse. She's an *"artiste"* all right, but not with the scissors! She takes a large hunk of my hair (I have a lot of hair) and pulls it towards her, and opens the scissors in the manner as if she is curling a ribbon. She drags the scissors along my hair while pulling my hair straight out from my head. Yank, pull, drag, chop, it seems to go on forever.

I emerged from the salon looking like a Beatle from the sixties. I bear a striking resemblance to Paul on the cover of the *Meet the Beatles* record album. The haircut looks good on Paul, me—not so much. The boys exclaim at my ugliness when we leave the hair salon, I kindly let them know that mommy isn't worried because her hair grows very quickly. Secretly, I regret my impulsive decision to go ahead with the *"artiste/chopper"* because my parents arrive tomorrow from the United States. I'm sure they'll be so glad to see us, that my shearing will escape their notice. In hindsight, I should have overruled the hair butcher and her blathering about her prowess as an *"artiste,"* thusly avoiding the porcupine look-alike contest.

After the shearing, we arrive home in the usual haphazard manner, the kids are thrown hither and yon in the backseat as I dodge various potholes and chickens in the road. When we arrive home unscathed (my children screaming with fear in the backseat), my supportive spouse greets me with hysterical laughter. He says he will "capture the moment for future reference." I can only imagine what he's up to; I put my foot down, (one picture only) thanking my lucky stars that my impulsive behavior doesn't include cranberry hair-color also.

Visitors

My parents arrived at the Nice airport several hours ago, not that they called, calling would be completely out of character for them. They rented a car at the airport and explored the countryside for three or four hours before arriving at our home. The way mom tells the story, they lost their way. Not surprising considering the lack of organized street signs. The roundabouts are very clearly marked, but these only get you to the town, the rest is up to the driver. My father has a good sense of direction however his erring ability to hit garbage containers and all existing potholes makes for a stressful journey (as reported by my mom).

When at long last they arrive, we all clamor around them for news from the states and the updates concerning 9/11. Being overseas, we feel left out and their reports bring us some sense of home.

Later, at dinner in Rick and Shannon's new home, the kids are overjoyed to see their grandparents. They miss familiar faces and grow tired of their boring parents.

We settle down outside on Rick and Shannon's veranda to enjoy a peaceful pre-dinner drink, the six kids holler and yell in the background, and the whirling of the contractor's buzzsaw invades the tranquil setting as he finishes up the "punch list" on their new rental home. A gnarly old fellow, wearing pants that only plumbers and teenage boys find attractive, and his friend with few teeth, appear in the front yard. He's carrying a piece of metal fence. Another man with even fewer teeth joins him. They start to drill holes into the cement directly in front of us. A high-pitched drill, not unlike the drill in the dentist office, now accompanies the whirring saw. Neither the workers nor Rick and Shannon exchange words as Plumber Pants and Toothless create an orchestra only recognized and loved by contractors at 7:00 in the evening.

Rick gets very red in the face and makes a beeline for Plumber Pants and his friend, Toothless. The French men don't understand Rick's garbled French but I feel sure they comprehend his gestures, although they ignore him. Toothless continues drilling while Rick puts in a call to the landlord of their rental home. Fortunately, Rick gets through, holds the phone outside, the homeowner can't mistake the shrill noise of the drill. After the landlord communicates with Plumber Pants, the solemn workers depart as quickly as they arrive.

I later found Rick outside practicing yoga moves in an unsuccessful attempt to calm his shattered nerves. I feel rather sorry for Rick and Shannon, as the "punch list" construction has been an ongoing project since they arrived in late August. The French laborers work at their own convenience, which never seems to be convenient for the homeowner or renter.

I Still Hate Horses

My sister loves to ride horses. I'm deathly afraid of horses mostly because of that long ago terrifying ride on her nag, Bravo, but for some reason, I offered to take riding lessons with her. Though I sincerely believe the horse isn't and never will be a friend of mine; maybe things will be different this time around. We mutually decide to try English riding lessons as opposed to Western. Shannon reports she is already an expert at Western based on her experience with her childhood pony.

Shannon earlier arranged a meeting with the instructor and I arrived first. I have a great amount of trouble communicating to the riding instructor. Apparently another American called this morning to cancel her lesson. The instructor glares at me and inquires in strident French, *"Pourquoi êtes-vous ici si vous êtes malade?"* My now well-tuned French ear heard: "Why sick?" I have no idea what he is talking about. I lose my focus due to his very tight white riding pants; I can't concentrate on his words. I'm too busy wondering if all instructors dress in such provocative clothing. Our conversation doesn't progress past my unobtrusively staring at his obviously underwear-less white pants until my sister arrives to rescue me. The instructor's body-hugging riding pants also distract Shannon. We discuss his unfortunate fashion choice thoroughly as we walk to the stables; she agrees he isn't wearing underwear. It must be a French thing.

After this auspicious beginning, we arrive at the stables to choose our steeds. Several very large rats scurry out of our path leaving me wondering about the cleanliness of the horses' stalls. Shannon says, not to worry, there are always rats at stables. I'm not convinced of this. The horses in the barn hang their heads out of their stalls, perhaps waiting for a carrot or a nibble on an unsuspecting visitor. Why can't they stay inside their own houses? They must be desperate for some company or an apple at the very least. Monsieur Tight Pants (as I now think of our riding instructor,) picks out a horse well-known for its smooth gait and gentleness for Shannon.

In contrast, my nag is shaggy with very large teeth to match his excessive girth. Attempting to calm myself, I conjure up a vision of a friendly plow horse. The instructor hands us brushes and the gear necessary to ride. My attempt at putting imaginary plow horse clothing on a wild stallion fails miserably and I beg Shannon to trade horses, but she is too afraid of Monsieur Tight Pants to trade nags.

As I attempt to brush my shaggy mount from the outside of the stall, the owner looks at me as though I've lost my mind. My parents, who accompanied us for some good humor and sure-fire entertainment, take pictures. Monsieur Tight Pants helps me saddle my old nag while shaking his head at his hopeless pupil. As I lead the horse outside, I'm grateful he doesn't step on my feet as I assumed he would. Seeing an opportunity to embarrass me, my dad takes additional candid shots of "inept daughter walking beast to the ring." The flash on the camera spooks my horse, they are less than helpful. I shout at him (my dad, not the nag) to mind his own business and "doesn't he know he has now spooked the horse."

Managing to mount my extremely tall charger without embarrassing myself is quite a feat, no stepstool required. We try something called "posting," I don't have the correct rhythm. The other students are posting with ease while I'm jostled from side to side, panting and sweating. My dad shouts at me to "post faster", I follow his instructions and it helps. He snaps another picture.

As I pull over to *"restez"* (remain or stay still) from posting, my plow horse sees sudden appeal in chomping on the dirt. I fight a losing battle to get his head up. Monsieur Tight Pants tells me to get a life or at least this is what I imagine he said, as his face is now purple with rage. The rest of the class begins to gallop, Monsieur Tight Pants resignedly tells me to *"être calme"* (be calm). Old "dirt eater" sees an opportunity to chew the non-existing grass again as I battle him for control of the reins. I really don't like my horse now because he wisely figured out I'm not the master. I'm not sure if this riding thing is for me and I still don't like horses. I lack the appropriate attire and what is the use of this riding business if you don't have a fetching outfit?

• • •

Craig's Observations

Shawn told me about the horse ride and I saw the resulting haircut. To date, she has been so proud of her French communication skills, but I must set the record straight on these "incidents," as painful as it is. She has repeatedly scoffed at my hand gestures mode of communication with the locals, a tried and true method. You do not see me walking around with a hedgehog haircut.

I have attached three photos below that are worth a thousand words each. Here is how the pictures are related and the "real story" of what happened rather than the fantasy story that Shawn would have you believe.

As you may surmise from Shawn's story, *"cheveux"* (hair), *"cheval"* (horse), *"chèvre"* (she-goat) are dangerously close in spelling and pronunciation. I avoid the risks of mispronouncing these words with simple hand gestures, although one fellow mistook my charade for horse as a she-goat, but no harm came of it. Anyway, Shawn wanted to go to horse-riding school with her sister, Shannon. Shawn does not like horses and is very nervous around them. When she arrived one-half hour early (you expect this from Shawn) at the stables, she tried to explain to the riding instructor (*sans* underwear, *avec* plumber butt) of her wishes. I offered to translate via hand gestures, but Shawn insisted on relying on her own method of verbal communication. The instructor understood her perfectly, but the correct translation was "I want a short haircut" instead of "I want a short horse ride." Fortunately for Shawn, the instructor also cuts hair as a hobby (the horses all have very nice haircuts), *"u n artiste"* he said. He proceeded to sit her down in an empty stall on a wooden stool and trim her hair. Shawn was fine with this, thinking it was necessary for her hair to fit in the jaunty helmet she must wear in the riding ring, (see first attached of jaunty helmet on Shawn). Fortunately, there are no mirrors at Salon de Horsefly, so Shawn is unaware of the disaster.

We arrive home, and I quickly snap a picture of Shawn's mowing, before her self-examination session with the mirror, screams, shrieks, etc. (see second picture).

Finally, in the third picture, you can find Shawn studying the book, *Communicate With Hand Gestures in 10 Minutes Per Day.*

• • •

Lost in Translation

After my communication issues with Monsiuer Tight Pants—my communication bravado dropped a level, however I still had the basic language skills my husband lacked. It's difficult for those new to the French language to discern the difference between hello, goodbye, and thank you. The English words translate into French as: *"bonjour", "au revoir",* and *"merci."* There's another word for goodbye, *"revoir",* and *"merci".* There's another word for goodbye, *"bonsoir",* which means good evening and is said anytime after five. Then, there is *"bonne nuit",* which means "good night". I can barely write all this now and keep it straight, although, at the time it seemed rather straightforward to me, in hindsight I may have been a bit delusional.

Craig, the self-proclaimed master of sign language, is forever saying, *"bonjour"* with a toothy grin after a waiter brings him an espresso. The correct response would of course be *"merci,"* not to be confused with, "mercy", which is a dead giveaway of your heritage.

We have friends from the United States visiting us for two weeks, they arrived shortly after Mom and Dad left. They have absolutely no French linguistic skills and must rely on Craig's method of communication/hand gestures. While our friend, John, and his son, Michael, have adopted Craig's method of communication, Robin, the most savvy of the three of them, greets Levio, the property manager each morning with hearty *"bonjour"* and says goodbye with an equally enthusiastic *"bonjour."* Levio cracks a rare smile but doesn't correct her mistake. I tactfully explain to Robin the difference in the salutations. Robin, being a quick study, does not make the mistake again. Craig continues to thank people with a happy *"bonjour";* he is still relying on his hand signals, which may be just the thing for him.

The Mushroom Hunt

Shannon belongs to the local library group; the patrons go on several outings a year. Shannon raves about the upcoming mushroom hunt. It was very popular last year, and I assume our guests will want to go on the hunt with us. Our fungus-finding guide speaks only French. Finding there is no English translator, the men in our group mention something about a preference for golfing; they're roundly ignored.

When we arrive at the assigned meeting area, an impressive group of elder book-reading French citizens happily greet us. Licky, Rick and Shannon's yellow lab, accompanies us, the French love all dogs. Licky is a definite "French-friend-magnet," useful in meeting people. I notice one fellow carries his *Flora and Fauna en Français* book with him, while some of the others wear all types of mushroom-hunting costumes. One elderly woman wears her blue dancing slippers while carrying a matching handbag. Her attire for our three-hour hike is a bit out of place unless she is going out for the evening after the hike. It's unfortunate that I can't explain to her in her native language the folly of such an outfit. Another fellow looks jaunty in his paisley printed silk tie and thin striped sport jacket; he rounds off the look with a walking stick. I certainly admire the way the French dress in their finery, no matter what the occasion. I do hope we're going to enjoy a magnificent mushroom feast after the hike with the accompaniment of white tablecloths to match our fellow hikers' attire.

The seven of us, out of a group of thirty or so, march off carrying a large picnic basket, but just as quickly decide to leave it in the car. It's too heavy for the three-hour journey. Our leader begins the hike at a brisk pace, and then suddenly stops within fifty feet to explain that today there are no mushrooms, but not to worry because she'll point out the large variety of woodland flora and fauna, lucky for the one fellow, who has the plant book. Judging by the downturned faces, I'm guessing my new French friends are just as disappointed as Shannon and I. The French can sometimes have rather dour expressions so the crabby look isn't too unusual. In our small group of seven, only Shannon and I understand the implications of what the leader has explained to the group. We don't tell the men, as it's quite possible they'll turn back immediately.

We proceed fifty more feet and stop again; I catch every tenth word and can only imagine what my husband, Craig, must be thinking. Unable to understand our leader, because she's talking so fast, I think about our picnic basket and the enticing treats that await us at lunch. Robin shows great interest in all things the guide points out; she's a good ambassador for the rest of us. The brush-loving leader stops and starts for three solid hours. The leader tells us several times we will arrive at our destination in *"juste dix minutes"* (just ten minutes). She says there's a marvelous stone village at the end of our journey; at least, that is what I think she says. I can't imagine the location of this village, there's sagebrush and weeds as far as the eye can see.

Suddenly, wild mustangs gallop toward us. Remembering my earlier experience with the unkempt beasts at the riding stables, I dodge behind a rock. Blue Slippers, with the matching handbag, isn't quick enough. The mangy mustang tries to eat her handbag, but she bravely hits the horse on the muzzle with her purse and nimbly dashes after the rest of the group. The slippers must have some serious tread on the bottom.

Rick comments about our "endless journey, and when do we get to eat something?" I'm hoping no one understands his English, as both he and I get rather crabby and unreasonable when we're hungry.

We arrived at the "natural village" built of stone, but I'm now so grumpy than I can't appreciate the beauty of the rock pile. In reality, there's no village, only many large boulders, an amazing geological wonder, if one is interested in that sort of thing. Of course, there's no *boulangerie* (bakery) at the stone village, not even a vendor selling espressos. I'm now barn sour and in desperate need of some sustenance. Two of the old ladies are also confused about our destination; perhaps, they too have low blood sugar. They search for some convenient café to rest their weary bodies. It seems our flower-loving leader bamboozled the entire group. Our three-hour mushroom hike has turned into a three-hour slug-filled slog.

Because there isn't anything to see but giant stones, we ditch the group early and head back to the car and our snacks. Both Rick and I grouse loudly as some of the other brown-nosers in the group make the expected awe-inspired gasping noises exclaiming over the natural beauty of the pile of rocks. Forty-five minutes later back at the car we unwrap our bountiful feast. We gorge upon baguette sandwiches, fresh fruit, and cheese from the market. Craig makes noises about having the final say on all future day trips. I ignore him. He organized our last hike where we ended up at the dump.

Water Anyone?

Well, for today and many other days, we're suddenly without water. Having recently returned from a sweat-producing bike ride, I'm ready for a refreshing shower. Unfortunately, a mere trickle dribbles from the showerhead when the faucet is turned on to full-blast.

In our neighborhood, the water doesn't always appear when one turns on the tap. If the water company needs to turn off the water due to the incessant construction in our neighborhood, then, they do so. No notification is necessary or expected by the French residents, they're all used to this procedure.

Recalling that I witnessed various ongoing construction projects when peddling out of my neighborhood, I realize this is most likely the reason for the lack of water. The water will be turned off for several hours or perhaps for most of the day. We adjust to the lack of water by simply jumping in the pool for a pseudo bath. Fortunately, Levio cleans the pool regularly, and we only lack some soap and shampoo. Of course, the toilets remain unflushed, but then this isn't anything new in our house. Despite dire threats from us, the boys seem incapable of flushing toilets here and in the United States. Perhaps this will change if the water is turned off for several days or more, at which point we will need to start carrying buckets of water from the pool, in order to flush the toilet.

～Part IV ～

From Treading Water to Swimming

Kids Terrorized on School Bus

The kids continue to flourish in their studies at school. The International School of Nice isn't as rigorous as my children's parochial school at home, therefore making their transition that much easier. Every day after we pick the kids up at the bus stop, we listen to accounts of the battles on the deluxe bus that transports them to and from school.

The bus monitor isn't a paid teacher as reported by the principal, but an upper-grade student. The International School of Nice pays said student to monitor the savages that ride the school bus. It's obvious to us and the other parents we talk to that this system isn't working. The kids are exposed to swearing and necking in the back of the bus on a daily basis, while some of the caffeine-charged kids run up and down the aisles. My oldest son, Austin, was forced to take on an older student who badgered his little cousin daily. We appointed Austin the designated bodyguard to his little cousins. I think he rather likes the position, being given full authority to mete out punches with a smack down if necessary. Letters to the principal produce no action. It's every child for himself on the hour-long ride.

Super Fun Happy Resort—Ibiza

The kids have an unexpected break and we (both families) are going to take a holiday at Super Fun Happy Resort, Ibiza, Spain. SFHR is a great solution when traveling with small children. There is often a "tykes club" that keeps small children occupied for most of the day. We procured rooms at the last minute because the travel industry has significantly declined here in Europe since 9/11.

On the morning of our departure, we arrived at the airport with time to spare. No employee stands behind the Air Liberal counter, as customer service isn't a French "custom."

Although I hate checking my luggage in case my bags get lost, it's necessary to check luggage when traveling with a family of five. I observe some people gathering at the counter—I assume to check luggage, and feel compelled to join them. I detest this lemming-like behavior in myself, but I'm unable to stop my compulsion to be first in line. Therefore, I'm fairly near the front of the line when the airline staffer finally arrives (late) at the ticket counter. The employee opens up for business, the lemmings have multiplied, and I'm now at the back of the line. This pushing and shoving isn't at all unusual in France and is the accepted norm, but I've not adjusted to this unruly behavior. The French don't comprehend the meaning of the word "line" unless it literally means, "please draw a line on a piece of paper." The British, like the Americans prefer to form an orderly "queue," but here in France, forming a queue simply says, "I'm a foreigner in a foreign land."

I put my oldest son, Austin, to work holding my current spot, which is now in the back of the "line" while I move to another area of the "line," in hopes of procuring a better position closer to the front. I take stock of those close to me so as not to lose my place. A man in a shiny black leather jacket moves in on me from the side, and I'm shoved further back. I curse under my breath (in French, of course) and attempt to knock into his Achilles tendon with my overloaded cart. I shout to Austin, "Every man for himself" and make like a French citizen and push my way to the front of the line. Austin pays me no heed and continues to read his magazine with his elbows resting casually on the cart. He's so like his father, who is currently lounging on a nearby couch while reading *The International Harold Tribune*. They're both oblivious to my self-imposed line stress. Conner takes over for his lame brother and boldly pushes his cart past all mothers and children as well as the man in the black jacket.

Finally, Craig ambles up to the counter, after observing us getting ready to check our luggage. "I'll handle it from here." "Fine, I'll hold your seat on the couch," I snidely remark, although in hindsight, his solution of waiting until the crowd cleared now seemed a better plan.

A short plane trip later, we arrived at Super Fun Happy Resort, which isn't anything like the pictures. We expected beachfront rooms and several luxurious pools. In reality the beachfront rooms are closed for renovations and only one pool remains open. There are mysterious bugs floating on the surface. The heat is turned off in the pool, and it's overcast and chilly. Many of the activities touted in the brochure are *"termine"* (finished) because it's the end of the busy season. The rooms are dismal, with a single light bulb hanging over single metal beds covered by dubious-looking "white" blankets. The walls are a canvas of mosquito bodies in various states of death.

We wake the next morning to the grinding and spraying of a giant tractor filled with pesticide. The machine dispenses a noxious spray from the rear of the equipment, destroying all living creatures in its path. Apparently, resort officials are trying to rid the place of guests as well as mosquitoes. Another tried and true method of giving us "the brush-off" includes a virtually empty gift shop. Apparently restocking the shop with the various sundries that travelers forget (toothpaste, ibuprofen) takes a backseat to customer service.

More Line Challenges and Language Difficulties

Each day at Super Fun Happy Resort we're subjected to more line aggravation, or lack of civilized queues. Leslie waits patiently each morning in the breakfast line.

She prepares her toast, which pops up only to have a woman come up behind her and grab it. She is seven and at a loss as to what action to take. I advise her to bite the next person who cuts in front of her and tries to steal her food. Every man, woman, and child are for themselves here at SFHR, this includes the tempting *pain au chocolate* croissants. No one bakes a better baguette or croissant than the French. Even though we're on the island of Ibiza off the coast of Spain, the cook is obviously French as is all of the staff. Every morning, the remaining guests at the club wait for the arrival of the delicious dark chocolate filled buttery croissants. One fluffy little boy in particular diverts my attention from the baked goods, because he so obviously has a passion for the breads. As I said, he is perhaps eight or nine, but he has the strength of two grown men as he shoves his way to front of the line each morning to grab a fist-full of the croissants. I looked for his parents, thinking perhaps they might reprimand his unruly behavior. No such luck, his porcine actions continue each morning.

My language difficulties continue at Ibiza. A very friendly staff member offered Craig and me a tasty poolside snack of fresh watermelon. I responded in French with a hearty, *"Je t'aime et vos pastèques."* Craig asks me, "What on earth did you say to him?" Not at all dismayed I reply to Craig what I think I said, "I love watermelon." Craig continues to comment aloud at the strange faces the waiter makes. Shannon, sitting next to us, is privy to the entire exchange. According to her, I said, "I love you and your watermelons." No wonder the waiter left in such a dither. Still part of me wonders if he is excited by my admiration of his watermelons.

The Hippie Market

Shannon and I expected to find a bit more shopping on the island of Ibiza than the "Hippy Market" the resort staff directed us to. The one remaining front desk employee actually referred to the market, as "The Hippie Market," I'm not sure what the actual name of the market is. It's here that my language problems run amuck again. French is the preferred language at SFHR, however in the streets of Ibiza, Spanish is spoken. Frustrated with my French language abilities, I decided to give Spanish a try; after all I did take Spanish for several years at Highland Junior High. After walking by stalls of hash pipes, water bongs, and tie-dyed rags posing as clothing, I confidently asked the jewelry vendor in Spanish, "How old is your jewelry?" It's obvious to anyone that I'm asking if the jewelry is antique. He cheekily replies in English, "I don't know how old the jewelry is, but I'm 44 years old." Sigh. My old junior high school Spanish isn't quite as polished as I thought.

The Climbing Wall

T he rough seas prevent us from scuba diving at Super Fun Happy Resort. Eager for a new adventure while the smaller children are occupied in the tyke's camp, we decide to join Austin and Conner at the climbing wall. The boys brag about their prowess as great climbers every afternoon.

Once at the wall, everyone is afraid to go first, so we opt for the time-honored decision-making method of "rock-paper-scissors." My sister loses. She straps on the pseudo cod-piece (the climbing harness) and the climbing shoes. She scales the rock like a lizard and Rick, Tom, and I follow suit. This is the easy section.

The Climbing Wall Again . . .

T he next day we meet at the climbing wall again, hooked with the heady success of yesterday. Shannon again scales the wall first. She is climbing well until she tries a tricky maneuver and falls off. Luckily, the sturdy line supports adult climbers. After Shannon's failure, I approach the wall with some trepidation, Shannon is sure if I say; *"Je suis le mur,"* or, "I'm the wall," my climbing skills will improve. The instructor cocks his head at me in a funny way, I wonder if I said *"Je suis le mur"* correctly. Knowing my sister, she may have directed me to say an inappropriate phrase. Anyway, the sentence brought me luck because neither I nor the men fall off the wall.

After leaving the younger climbers at the wall, we congratulate ourselves by downing several beers; we're climbers in our own minds.

Still Climbing . . .

We head back the next day, a bit sore from repeated leg extensions, but ready for more climbing. The instructor informs us of an ensuing contest. This puts an entirely different spin on things, not the French against the Americans, but pitting the young against the not-so-young climbers. We can laugh at ourselves, but what if one of the youngsters recognizes us for the pretenders we actually are.

All of the contestants scale the first section of the wall, and then the second wall easily. Unfortunately, I'm the first to fall off the third wall. Not only is this humiliating as I dangle precariously down the side of the wall, I also knock myself silly when I hit my head while swinging back and forth on the rope. Shannon is nearly doubled over in hysteria, as are my boys. Bad karma comes to those who laugh at others and Shannon loses her battle with the wall. The instructor allows her a second attempt to haul her rear-end over the difficult bit, but she fails miserably. Another humiliation for the "not-so-young contenders," however Craig and Rick save our team as they succeed at the third wall.

Four contestants remain; Rick and Craig must maintain the honor of the "not-so-young" team by scaling the fourth wall. This section has a large over-hang, which they must somehow scramble up. Rick gives it his best shot. He swings back and forth on the rope to gain enough momentum to place him higher than the overhang. While Rick does manage to grapple the overhang with one foot, the remainder of his body dangles down the side. The crowd cheers his efforts. Craig is next; he simply uses brute strength to scale the wall but can't heave his butt over the protruding ledge. He plunges down the face, while the rope screams shrilly through the pulley. After the failed attempts of the "not-so-young," a young boy succeeds with many leaps and bounds, and I impulsively shout in French, *"Vous êtes la grenouille!"* (You are the frog!)

He DOES have a habit of leaping! Shannon says in a loud stage whisper, perhaps this isn't the best term to use with our French friends for obvious reasons. I don't mean to be insulting to the successful climber. It's just that one must be able to cling like a barnacle and leap like a frog in order to scale a steep rock wall, and I don't know the French word for barnacle.

• • •

Craig's Observations on Our Vacation

No one has said anything to me since we arrived back in France on Saturday, but, I'm pretty sure my suspension from picking vacation spots is final. My good intentions paved the way to a week in Hell. It was the children's week off from school; every school in

France was out on vacation. We traveled to a big rock in the Mediterranean off the coast of Barcelona called Ibiza. The brochure met all of the adult criteria: scuba diving, rock climbing, sailing, golfing, even horse riding for Shawn and Shannon. The brochure met all of the children's criteria: Tyke club with tons of supervised activities. Just a few defects knocked the place off the five-star list: lack of potable water in the taps and bottled water was available at your expense only, nasty sewer smell near the swimming pool, armies of biting bedbugs, an air force of pigeons and their droppings from roosting on the balconies at night, and so much more. My vacation mates still won't look me in the eye.

We did have some laughs, however. Shawn, trying to use her best Spanish, was a great ambassador for our nation. We went shopping for a few hours at the "hippie market". This is a collection of trash that some smart entrepreneur hauls out of a warehouse once a week for the tourists to fawn over and pay 500% more than it is worth. My brother-in-law noted that there were five merchandise groups: tie-dyed clothes, silver (tin) jewelry, wooden voodoo masks, bongs, and velvet pictures. Ironically, every fifth table had the clothing, followed by a jewelry table, etc. Shawn and Shannon did not notice this pattern over the span of about two hundred tables, believing this event to be shopping Heaven (in vacation Hell.) It isn't possible for Shawn to walk through one of these markets without buying something. This time it was Campbell's Soup cans posing as rings and bracelets. She was a little overconfident with her Spanish language, however, when she inquired about the cost of a particularly fetching bracelet made from either a tomato or mushroom can (judging by the smell). Unfortunately, she asked how old the bracelet was. The dread-locked dude looked confused for a minute, collected his cannabis-fogged thoughts, then answered that he did not know how old the precious trinket was but that he was forty-four years old. That was good enough for her, she happily paid full price.

When back in the confines of the "luxury resort," Shawn switched from Spanish back to using French. A young stud muffin waiter was walking by the pool, handing out slices of watermelon on one of the few warm afternoons. Shawn thought she said; "I love watermelon!" to our new French friend wearing a Speedo two sizes too small. Unfortunately, the correct translation was, "I love you and your watermelons." He looked nervous, nodded and ran off. We didn't see him again and the free watermelon samples were cancelled for the remainder of the vacation. I was mystified by his reaction; the typical male would take this as the highest form of flattery, even if accidental. I learned later that a drought had decimated the watermelon crop in Ibiza this year and the fruit was growing only to five percent of normal size.

Finally, we tried a new sport while in Ibiza, wall climbing. We came up with some great nicknames associated with activity. Shawn is "Be the Wall;" Shannon is "The Eagle," signifying her ability to fly up the wall; Rick was the "The Rabbit," testifying to his ability to hop effortlessly from ledge to ledge. Unfortunately, my nickname was the "The Camel" because of my unorthodox climbing style whereby my hindquarters stuck out 3-4 feet from the wall. This isn't textbook climbing, according to the spotters. I was eliminated early on in the climbing contest at the end of the week. However, my redemption occurred that evening in the bar, when I congratulated the very buff winner of the climbing contest. I said in perfect English, "Congratulations on a spectacular win today." He was French and understood not one word I said, but when I gave him the thumbs up and mimed a rock climber, he understood immediately and gave me a big smile and reached out and firmly (crushingly) shook my hand. Once again, Craig, the hand signaler, prevails over Shawn, the language poser, on international communications.

. . .

Olive Oil Anyone?

T he property caretaker, Levio, is neglecting our olive trees, and the olives are in desperate need of picking. Our other neighbors are currently harvesting their olives, while our fruit withers on the trees.

We have an abundance of olive trees on the property and no olive oil. I tried to communicate this to Levio; he looked at me impassively and asked his helper to speak to me. After conferring with Levio, the tall gangly helper explained, *"Nous sélectionnons des olives dans une semaine"* (We select olives in one week). I hope the olives survive another week, but then I don't know much about olive orchards. Levio speaks a combination of French and Italian and is virtually impossible to understand, even hand signals don't work with him. I'm beginning to get a complex with my inability to communicate with my French friends, but most especially with Levio.

Apparently, the landlord also wants the olives harvested because Levio starts work the following day after speaking to the landlord by phone. Levio refuses my help with the olive picking. He and his helper put large nets under the trees and proceed to whack the branches with long sticks to dislodge the now bruised olives. I wondered aloud at Levio and his assistant's method of de-oliving the trees. They either don't hear me or they just ignore me. Next, Levio loads the bushels of olives in his truck and the kids and I happily follow him down the road to the olive *presse*. I managed to convey our desire to follow him with a pantomime of driving the car and pointing at him. The olive *presse* is a giant ancient looking stone wheel used to literally press the juice out of the olives, a very simple but effective method to procure olive oil. The *presse* is lodged in an old stone building with a heavy barn door. It's fortunate we arrive early for the olive pressing because the line extends out the door by the time we've finished. It takes many olives to make two 5-gallon liters of olive oil. The operator claims our orchard owner usually takes only the first press or the virgin olive oil. The olive oil is at first a bright green color when bottled; the yellow color that we see in stores is actually aged olive oil. As I taste a bit of the oil, my face reflects the sharpness of the bright green liquid. Perhaps Levio didn't appreciate being badgered to harvest the olives, but we enjoyed the process of watching the olives move from the trees into bottles of oil.

Currently, our olive oil resides in giant glass containers in a dark cellar where Levio checks on it daily. The owner of our rented villa bottles and privately labels the oil into kitchen-sized containers to send to his friends.

The last time I spoke to Björn he asked me what labels I was going to put on my bottles of olive oil. This has me very excited indeed, just thinking of all the clever names I could come up with. "You can't claim the oil as your own, Shawn, for God's sake we're only renting the place." I'm currently considering the name, "Pepito's Oil". I'm sure I'll gain some points with Levio if I name the olive oil after the neighborhood cat. He loves that cat.

Florence

R ick, Shannon, Austin, and I are very excited about going to Florence, Italy. Sadly, Craig isn't able to go to Florence because of business issues in the United States. We leave the five other children in Crystal's capable hands, although it's necessary to increase her pay after her last babysitting experience with Leslie and Conner.

We decided to drive to Florence rather than take the train, and in hindsight, I know a direct train ride would have been the wiser choice. The Italians are even worse drivers than the French, if that's possible. While negotiating the four-lane, sometimes two-lane road to Florence, one is apt to come across many long tunnels. The tunnels are sometimes five miles long. Apparently, a lot of crashes occur in these tunnels and right outside the tunnels, where one is nearly blinded entering the bright sunlight from the miles-long tunnels.

Austin is my co-pilot in the car. He's supposed to read the map and keep an eye out for road signs to Florence. He exclaims over the cool Jaguar rather close to us on the freeway, but continually forgets to look for signs and dangers on the road. Everyone in the car grows frustrated with Austin's attention lapses so we fire him from his job as co-pilot. He's relegated to the back seat where he happily prattles away about the passing sights.

Shannon planned the entire trip and weeks earlier acquired reservations at Hotel Magnifico. This is the real name of the hotel. The description in no way described the broken down building we finally locate miles from the heart of the city. It's a 45-minute walk to central Florence. Rick and Shannon's room is located in the attic, which requires Rick to walk in a stooped position. Austin and I share a double-sized very lumpy bed with a bathroom down the hall. Shannon exclaims over the great accommodations. The rest of us remain silent.

As is customary in most European hotels, breakfast is included in the room charge. In the breakfast room the following morning, we locate a couple of cellophane packaged biscuits left for us on the table. Tea bags remain unused because of lack of hot water. Even Shannon isn't happy with the breakfast presentation.

During "breakfast," Shannon is delegated as our representative to inform the hotel owners that we're only staying one night instead of the three nights previously booked. "I can't do it, they were so nice, and what excuse will I give them?" Shannon is greeted with silence from our unhappy group and she musters up the courage to inform the landlords of our impending departure.

A ten-minute drive finds us in the heart of the city. As we start our walking tour, the Hotel Savoy looms large and inviting. After a quick one-minute discussion, we relocate to the Hotel Savoy in downtown Florence. Austin says, "This is more like it."

As our tour guide, my sister keeps us busy for the entire day; there's so much to see in Florence. Our first stop, Il Duomo, is a cathedral with a domed roof, which took one hundred and seventy years to complete. Climbing to the tiptop of the dome is an exercise in patience . . . not that I mind huffing up four hundred plus stairs, in an extremely narrow and steep stairway, which has miniature barred windows. I quickly learn to look forward, as looking backwards causes extreme vertigo, a quick view out the very tiny windows along the climb leaves me feeling rather anxious about the immense height we have scaled thus far.

Near the top, and still inside of Il Duomo, we walked around the gorgeous unprotected frescoes on some sort of painter's scaffolding. Touching the artwork is possible, but not advisable. Ruining the great works of art with fingerprints would follow me to my grave.

On the very top and outside of Il Duomo, Austin's hot chocolate suddenly begins to work on his system. A steaming cup of Italian hot chocolate is similar to a bowl of hot pudding, the effects of which left Austin dancing about like a young gazelle on a sugar cane high. He pranced and cavorted around the fenced cupola (a mere million foot drop over the edge) until I nearly fainted with anxiety. All of this leaping about greatly amuses the nearby Italians who make jokes to Austin. They love kids, even big gangly youths. The wind is fierce, forcing me to sit on the extreme back edge by the wall until Rick and Shannon finish taking their pictures.

Much to Rick's dismay, our tour guide (Shannon) thoughtfully scheduled time for shopping. Shannon and I (Rick wisely finds a café to spend his time) peruse the various leather shops, purchasing an entire cow in the form of two pair of boots, two coats, two handbags and three belts. Austin's agenda differs from ours.

While wandering the ancient streets of Florence, my thirteen-year-old son spots a Nike Shop. After much discussion, we agree to accompany him inside the shoe mecca. Austin exits the store an hour later wearing royal blue patent leather Nikes. He's beside himself with joy as he works on perfecting his gazelle-like leaps about the streets of Florence. "I'm going to be awesome in the school basketball tournament." He says with glee. The leather capital of the world and he buys patent leather high tops. Perhaps, when we arrive home and he begins his "shoe pay-off", (babysitting his cousins and siblings) his joy will not be as pure, but for now he's in heaven.

We've truly enjoyed our stay in Florence with the sights so easily accessible, and Botticelli paintings living in the open and not under Plexiglas. The Italians are such a different animal than the French, the countries so close in proximity, and yet the people of Italy and France are as different as night and day. The French, although friendly in a stilted sort of way, don't have the same openness as the Italians. When entering an Italian eatery, whether it's a fine restaurant or a small back alley café, one immediately feels welcome, like a member of the family. Happy greetings from a flirtatious waiter or a rotund owner/chef shouting a hearty *buon giorno* from the back of the open kitchen are typical. There are simply no people more gracious than the Italians. Yes, we're sad to leave Italy.

No Turkey For You

It's no easy task to procure a frozen or, heaven forbid, a fresh turkey in the south of France. Thanksgiving is an American tradition and not a recognized French holiday; I don't recall any stories of pilgrims feasting with Native Americans in France. Shannon and I talked to friends and researched possible turkey locations. We must locate a turkey for Thanksgiving and the upcoming *fête* or festival at The International School of Nice. If we're lucky enough to find a turkey for Thanksgiving, the Thanksgiving holiday is a sort of turkey-cooking trial for the upcoming *fête*, when people other than family members will actually pay to eat our prepared feast.

At a grocery in Antibes, known for its English/American products, I attempted to communicate our needs to the grouchy clerk in the meat department, while Shannon scoured the aisles filled with Nutella and Spam. The French word for turkey is *dinde*, I used the word *dinde* in as many sentences as my limited language abilities allowed. *"Vous avez une dinde à vendre?"* (Have you a turkey for sale?) *"Où la dinde habite?"* (Where does the turkey live?) *"Vous avez oiseau plus grand le poulet?"* (Have you bird bigger than chicken?) And finally *"Êtes-vous une dinde?"* (Are you a turkey?) Of course, I didn't really say the last line but I wanted to. Finally, I resorted to bouncing around and flapping my arms while making what I must say are unparalleled gobbling sounds. I have always been a talented method actor, and this method worked. The linguistically challenged clerk ordered us one giant turkey, not two small turkeys as I hoped. It's difficult to mime two turkeys dancing about. According to the clerk, the monster turkey resides in another store in a distant village, most likely a leftover frost burned victim from some homesick American from years gone by.

The following day, Rick and Shannon try to pick the turkey up from the remote town the clerk referred to. Shannon's story about the turkey-fetching differs from mine.

• • •

Shannon's Turkey Recap

You were too "busy" to pick up the turkey because you planned a spa pedicure and a massage on the day we were to pick up the turkey. Rick and I (he was forced to come with me because the stores were difficult to locate) drove to three English/American stores (a chain) looking for the elusive bird, finally, we found it in the original store in Antibes. The clerk hadn't understood your gobbling after all and thought you wanted to pick up the carcass in another store. Not only did we waste three hours as we drove around, but we got lost four times.

• • •

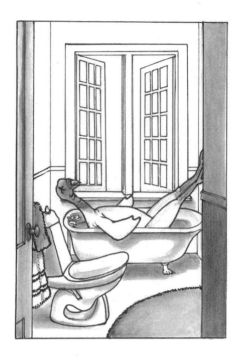

The turkey is purchased in the early morning hours (early for the French, 10:00 AM.) The fowl is covered in ice, a solid beast of a bird wearing a grimace on his still attached frozen head, while unmoving feet stick out of the end of the bag. One hundred Euros trades hands and the three of them drive home with the heat turned on high in hopes of thawing out the iced-over carcass.

Back at Rick and Shannon's home, the sink proves too small for the giant bird. Ever resourceful, Shannon resorts to filling the bathtub with hot water to warm up old frozen claws for our upcoming Thanksgiving dinner.

For some reason the frozen turkey incident is my fault. My hair and massage appointment conflicted with my appointment to pick up the bird, thus the fowl duty fell to Rick and Shannon. According to Shannon, I have the attitude of some sort of bon-bon eating princess when in reality my massage and nail appointment were previously scheduled at the same hour.

Just bad timing.

We invited our friends Susan and her daughter, Kate, from the International School of Nice to join us for the Thanksgiving feast. Susan, boasting she never cooks, treats us to one of her rare specialties, mashed potatoes with at least six pounds of butter. It must be a southern thing, she is from Alabama. The creamy white potatoes go elegantly with the stuffing prepared by Shannon and the usual accompaniment of vegetables. The fifteen-pound turkey, having spent two days in the bathtub, finally thawed enough to enter the oven.

Fortunately, Giselle, Rick and Shannon's housecleaner, consents to help with the dinner. Obviously, the French don't celebrate the American holiday of Thanksgiving, and she is intrigued by the whole idea. Although the oven isn't antiquated like the oven I attempted to use in our first house, it is a British model. The British oven doesn't faze Giselle, she somehow squeezes the bird in the smallish oven and the smells of home permeate the kitchen.

Of course, the dinner conversation revolves around the hunt for the turkey and a demonstration of my method acting. Our guests look suspiciously at the bird with its now removed appendages as we relate the state the bird arrived in. In hindsight, perhaps not the best dinner conversation.

• • •

Craig's Observations on the Birthday Party

This evening, the children are attending a birthday party at Stars and Bars, the famous American restaurant/bar in the harbor at Monte Carlo. Stars and Bars is a substantial upgrade over birthday parties at Chuck E. Cheese as it's in the shadow of the Royal Palace and one hundred and fifty-foot mega-yachts across the street in the harbor. As with all social events, we go along with them. We are desperate for other adult company; in fact, all of the parents stay for the entire party. They must also have no friends.

On the way home, we discussed maturity with our oldest son, Austin, who's almost thirteen. Austin is eager to earn money by babysitting his siblings and his cousins, when their parents are desperate to go out for an evening. The money is good for the work involved, and Austin has an overly high opinion of his job performance. We complimented him on his willingness to take on responsibility and save money as indications of his budding maturity.

Unfortunately, Austin has learned about the concept of credit and credit cards from his mother. He has had his eye on a pair of particularly fetching Nike basketball shoes for the last three months and, in a weak moment on the trip to Florence, he prevailed upon Shawn to front him the money to purchase the tools that make his game complete.

I was in Seattle during this trip to Florence, stocking up on Grape Nuts and Kraft Mac and Cheese for the family pantry. Had I been present for this purchase, Austin would doubtless still be wearing a malodorous pair of nondescript white basketball shoes purchased in the States. The Nikes are translucent blue, with a glow and shine much like the ruby slippers Dorothy wore in the *Wizard of Oz*. I don't believe Dorothy could dribble between her legs on the run or shoot lights out from the 3-point line, but then, neither can Austin.

I'm sorry to say, if I tried to borrow the same amount for a real estate project, my banker would ask me for some additional security, personal guarantees, and a car detailing. I watched Austin's basketball practice the next evening before the unveiling of the blue shoes, but, his game did not markedly improve relative to the great expectations the sapphire slippers created. His teammates gave him a good ration, leaving me free to keep my mouth shut and just smile on the sidelines.

Afterward, I asked him how he was going to pay Shawn back for the loan she had so loosely granted without a promissory note or credit check. He was miffed citing his big wad from babysitting. I pointed out he was less than one third of the way to the payoff for the shoes and he would need cash in the interim for other important activities. What about the school dances coming up? What money did he have to buy his date a corsage if it was all invested in basketball shoes? Certainly, he couldn't pin one of the Nikes on her dress and hope she would like the color or overlook the smell. He was not laughing.

He switched gears referring to the many ways he could earn money around the house. He offered to carry in groceries from the car, clean his room, do the dishes, pick up all the junk he left around the house, and many other necessary chores. I pointed out that he was already obligated to perform such work for free. His shoulders slumped, his head nodded back, and he recited his favorite sentence, "It's not fair." I have heard this many times before and have almost perfected an imitation of Austin reciting his favorite phrase. He isn't amused by my caricature.

I offered to purchase or lease the shoes from him so I could wear them in the annual Dads *vs.* senior high school basketball game this Saturday. I'm counting on the shoes to increase my vertical leap 100% from four to eight inches. I used to be able to jump much higher, but, with all of the biking I've been doing lately, apparently, I have trained different muscle groups. I'm sure Lance Armstrong would understand and agree. I also understand the Dads team has never lost the annual classic, so, there is real pressure involved. Confident that basketball was just like riding a bike after a twenty-year layoff, I went to the outdoor courts yesterday to practice with Austin and Conner and Rick. It became clear in three minutes that the blue shoes are not going to be enough to carry my game. I'm bedridden today, lying on an icepack and taking high doses of Aleve. I'm sure the Dads team needs a coach or manager with flashy looking shoes and I plan to apply for the job tomorrow.

• • •

French Class

R ick and I are struggling through French class once a week. One of our friends at The International School of Nice (our only source for friends, thus far) suggested we join her in a class to "improve" our French. Recalling the still recent turkey purchase incident, both Rick and I are understandably nervous. The varying accents in our little part of France make it increasingly difficult to speak the language, in some form, that the locals understand.

Our instructor, Jean François, is a very stilted French fellow who teaches classes in his home. Rick and I carpool from Grasse and the drive takes forty minutes, during which time we fret about possibly flunking the class before we have even started. All worries dissipate when we realize that we know the other five students in the class from the kids' school.

Before class, Rick and I catch up on all of the school gossip, making it worth the drive to the distant village. Our two hour class is exhausting. The best part of the morning is the break for tea and biscuits and juicy school gossip naturally follows a steaming cup of tea. Sometimes our instructor catches one of us off guard. He asks in a normal voice (as opposed to his slooow teaching voice.) *Quelle heure est-il?* or "What time is it?" Such an easy question, but we all look at him with uncertainty, until he pointedly looks at his watch. Seven light bulbs go off as his inept students slowly grasp the question being asked. The reason behind the quick (to our unpracticed ear) question, said at a normal French pace, is simple. Locals will know us for pretenders if we can't comprehend a simple question spoken in the rapid fire pace the French use. Fair enough.

After two weeks, we're dreading our French class (despite the morsels of information we pick up about the kids and the school in class). Rick says he is tired of conjugating verbs (at least he is proficient at it) and wants to practice and learn some new nouns to go along with his action verbs. *Bien joué* (well played) only goes so far in the real world. I'm beginning to think a more efficient means to practice the language requires interacting with the shop owners and the people in the village. The French really are very tolerant of my poor language skills because I'm trying to fit in. My sister practices at the local library in our neighborhood. It's a French/English "conversation group" that meets once a week. Perhaps, I'll try to horn in on her group, and it's free.

The Winter Fête

E very year the International School of Nice has a Winter *Fête* or festival. The purpose of the *Fête* is to earn money for the school. Apparently, the "out of country" tuitions (extravagant) are not sufficient. After four months, Conner still doesn't have an English book; maybe this extra money will be contributed to the "book procurement program." But whatever the reason for the *Fête*, we're unable to escape parent "volunteer hours" regardless of what country we live in. No *fête* is complete at an international school without foods from the cultures represented at the school. The event is similar to the "Bite of Seattle" but on a much smaller scale.

The parent-prepared food of the country sells at an astronomical price to the other "volunteer parent" *Fête* attendees and their children. After much debate, the team of Americans choose to prepare a turkey dinner, reminiscent of a Thanksgiving feast—a traditional American Holiday. Shannon and

I expressed our concerns over the dinner choice due to our previous experience with procuring and cooking a turkey. I'm simply not willing to gobble like a turkey again, and I know Shannon harbors a secret resentment because of "misunderstanding" over the turkey pick-up incident. We are outvoted.

At the *Fête,* the Italians sold pasta, the Germans sold Weiner schnitzel, and our turkey dinner is sold out! After so much trouble and preparation, we're overjoyed by our success. The varying groups decorated tables with the countries themes and symbols. Our table is a formal presentation with a white tablecloth, large candles bookmark each end and the center is covered with tempting dishes, surrounded by miniature pumpkins and baby corns.

Having bought, cooked, and prepared the side dishes before, Shannon and I have little trouble this time; however the other Americans suffered some paralytic catastrophes. Pam, a friendly soul hailing from Arizona, located turkey legs, but nothing else and presented her dish as a sort of turkey hash. Another American, Dede, doesn't have the fortitude to remove the turkey's feet and covers the cooked appendages in white paper frilly socks. The attendees don't seem to notice and devour all of turkey, mashed potatoes, stuffing, gravy, and vegetables. The smell of roasted turkey draws parents and guests from across the room and we can't serve the food fast enough. I'm terribly afraid the food isn't going to last through the event. I've secretly stashed away a plate for Craig who is outside practicing "hoops" for the upcoming seniors versus dads' basketball game.

The *fête* is very successful; there are booths for nail painting, tattoos, and even an exhibition of professional dirt bike riders. However, the real draw is the annual senior students versus school dads basketball tournament. The dads have an unbeaten record at the school thus far.

Austin (not old enough to play with the high school students) started as the assistant referee but is soon fired, as the "real referee" doesn't like his calls, which follow the rules. Austin is demoted to timekeeper, which suits him just fine. Austin (still going by the playbook) isn't told to keep the clock running each time the ball rolls out of the courts, so he stops the clock each time the ball rolls out of the court, or when there is a foul, he assumes he's supposed to keep time as it's done in a real game. Apparently, the "dad rule" requires Austin to keep the clock running. The game is SUPPOSED to have ten-minute quarters; this gives the dads, some of whom exhibit extra girth around the middle and rather slow footwork, a fighting chance. Again, Austin doesn't know these pre-determined rules.

The school does not have defibrillators on the grounds; the out-of-shape dads sweat heavily after the first half hour. Craig uses a never-seen-before maneuver for recovering the ball. He simply falls on one of the teenagers, thereby crushing the air out of his opponent's lungs; the ball is then easily grabbed. I've witnessed this move on WWF wrestling but never on a basketball court. Craig perfected this technique after the first half hour. After two hours, the game goes to overtime, the dads give in to exhaustion, and the seniors win. There's a rematch scheduled for the spring *fête*. This is the first time the dads lost the basketball game; some of the dads exhibit poor sportsmanship, blaming my son for his time-keeping.

We see several of the dads later, and they admit to heavy use of painkillers and ice. Perhaps in the re-match the men will have use of supplemental oxygen and Austin will not be the timekeeper.

On the drive home, Craig pleads exhaustion from the basketball game and hastens to his bed with some painkillers. A likely excuse, he simply doesn't want to go to the Christmas party this evening with Shannon, Rick, and me.

The party is at Mimi's home, a library group friend of Shannon's; she's the first in our little enclave to make some real French friends.

● ● ●

A French Christmas Party

Rick, Shannon, and I managed to find the party in the suburbs of Mougin with little problem. I'm sorry Craig elected to stay home, as I feel certain that his novel method of hand signal communication would have been a hit. Shannon neglected to tell me that the party is a gift-exchange so I arrived empty-handed.

Mimi greets us at the door wearing a gorilla mask, perhaps a costume leftover from Halloween, a holiday quickly gaining popularity here in France. Mask still intact, Mimi introduces us to some of the neighborhood locals, most of whom know Shannon from her French/English conversation class at the library. The library class guests are very interested to meet Rick and me, for the simple reason that we're Americans and good prospects for their library conversation group. After introductions they assure Rick and I that our French is very good indeed. We merely greeted them with a polite, "*Bonsoir,*" Rick and I can only assume they must be desperate for some more people who speak English.

We circulated around a bit, and after Rick conjugated a few verbs for the party guests (his specialty), we lost our luster as new and interesting visitors. Mimi intercepted our wandering and asked us to sit down. I noticed that indeed everyone is sitting, and we're chair-less. Miraculously no one is sitting by the fire, so we ensconce ourselves by the nice warm blaze and immediately feel uncomfortably warm from the fire as we politely try to decipher the language of the man next to us. He's French but lacks front teeth so he's a French mumbler, a trying situation under the best of circumstances. The three of us gracefully attempt to leave the awkward situation but Mimi sensing our departure (even if only to another hopefully vacant seat) instructs us to remain seated where we linger and baste by the fire. Finally a bell tinkles, at which point everyone rises to join a buffet line for dinner. Sweat is now dripping off my forehead and I have removed most of my unnecessary layers.

Amazingly there's no pushing and shoving in the buffet line for dinner. In my experience, pushing and shoving is normal French behavior. The influx of English guests may have created a more "civil" sort of line of hungry guests.

After bolting her food down, Shannon dashes to the restroom. Assuming there's some sort of emergency, I follow her. We leave Rick to baste his other side by the fire, and conjugate more verbs with Toothless.

It's understood in all countries that women go to the restroom in pairs. Usually some juicy bit of information needs to be discussed (in this case, our mumbling neighbor by the fire) and of course the facilities must also be used. Shannon completes her business all the while discussing Toothless and then attempts to zip up her new French couture pants. I try to help her with no success; no pliers (a useful tool for a stuck zipper) are available in the bathroom. I incorrectly assumed a French household would have pliers for ready access in the privacy of bedroom or bathroom as the French wear extremely tight pants.

Shannon somehow cobbles together her pants with a wooden clothespin she finds attached to the shower rod. Pulling her sweater over the lumpy front panel of her shiny couture pants, she shuffles crab-like (this is necessary to keep her pants from falling off her body) back out to the couch, where she thankfully collapses.

When we returned to the fire, Rick has sweat running down his face, either from the heat or from the stress of his attempts at conversation with the mumbler. As people begin to circulate, we take our cue and unglue ourselves from our chairs.

Some very amusing English people want Rick and me to join the library conversation group. "I can only speak cave-man French, a new abbreviated French language that's self taught," I say. They think I'm joking. "My specialty is conjugating verbs," says Rick. Our ever-present hostess, saves me from what I now assume is some sort of conversation-cult that meets at the library.

It's time for the holiday "sing-along."

All the guests grip several sheets of music as they look expectantly at the piano player. Am I in a 1950s musical? This party is completely surreal. Singing *Jingle Bells* and *Deck the Halls* in English certainly sounds amusing with the combined French and English accents. I add my own chorus of, *"ha, ha, ha"* after "laughing all the way" during *Jingle Bells*. The other guests are unaware of this line so I sing by myself.

Christmas Preparations

Rick, Shannon, Craig, and I managed to do a bit of Christmas shopping in London, England. The kids really are clamoring for the newest computer games and we want to see the first "Harry Potter" movie, a likely excuse for the forty-five minute plane ride across the channel.

Shopping in London is so festive with the trees glittering white fairy lights and the store windows gaily depicted holiday scenes. The crowds are huge, but none of us minds because it's so great to be surrounded by a language we completely (well, almost) understand. I guess we all have a touch of homesickness during the Christmas season. My parents arrive shortly after we return which, of course thrills all the grandchildren, I'm sure they are hoping for even more presents.

The Christmas holidays here in France are much the same as home, except we're blissfully uninvolved in (not invited to) the procession of parties that always accompany the holidays. Our Christmas decorations remained at home, not deemed essential when we packed for our yearlong venture, thus no tree festoons the living room which is better than the rather forlorn "Charlie Brown" trees we have seen in a few parking lots. A pathetic sight. Besides, we're leaving for a ski trip to Alpe d' Huez, on the 22nd of December. I'm looking forward to the ski trip, having spent Christmas in a French ski resort when my parents were living in Marbella, Spain with my sister.

Alpe d'Huez

It is an unseasonably dry year, and, the Alpe d' Huez ski resort is the one and only area in France with snow. Who cares if it is manmade? We are skiing in the Alps with millions of people who revel in pushing and shoving on the few snow-covered slopes available. Even though our last family vacation was a disaster at the Super Fun Happy Resort, we are gluttons for punishment—and the price is right.

Booking the trip at the travel agency in Nice required all my patience and some zen meditation. Cheerfully greeting the agent as we walk into the office, Shannon explains we have an appointment with the one agent who speaks English. She had called previously to insure that someone spoke English for the complicated transaction. The agent ignores this statement and gestures us to a desk. She isn't only rude but after she briefly helps us, she insists we sign a contract with extremely small print. Shannon asks again for the agent who speaks English because the contract is all in French and her French only applies to traffic signs and reading labels in the supermarket. The agent speaks only French and says, *"Vous retournez demain."* (You return tomorrow.) What a surprise, apparently she thinks we have nothing else to do during the busy Christmas season but drive forty-five minutes one-way into Nice to meet with an English-speaking agent. Just parking the minivan takes us thirty minutes. We have wasted our time with her and go out for lunch, determined to return tomorrow with a dictionary, if necessary.

Returning the next day produces a bit more of a positive outcome. Not only is Grouchy, the travel agent MIA, but an agreeable agent is most helpful and accommodating. We book our trip with to Alpe d' Huez without nearly the hassle we anticipated.

We leave the following week in a caravan of three vehicles. Rick and Shannon drive one car, while my parents drive their rented car and we, of course, are in the minivan. The drive is uneventful except that my parents stopped constantly for snacks.

Though the resort is great for keeping the kids occupied, they waiver on organizational skills. I stood in one endless line after another when we arrived. The French don't acknowledge lines, and so I stood in a sea of total confusion. Seven different times I waited with the masses for room keys, skis, boots, beads for drinks, etc. At the end of the sixth mass of people, I simply walked straight to the front of the "line" and asked the surprised man to fit my son's boots to his skis. It's so strange, but the French never say anything when one cuts to the front of the line. What are they going to say? They rightly assume you have reached your limit or you have a good reason for cutting the line—I've learned it's an unspoken rule, it's ok. My reason, should they have asked, is that I'm tired and hungry. Craig is perturbed with me because I'm not supposed to use the boys' personal skis. "Why didn't you use the rental skis instead of the boys' new skis? There are a lot of rocks on the hill." "Oh, I'm sorry, what were you doing while I was waiting in line?" I astutely ask. He's studiously quiet after that. He hates waiting in line as much as I do.

Boarding the gondola requires some stepping on skis in order to manage any headway in the "line." Once in the gondola, claustrophobia is a very real possibility as the crush of muffled, zippered, gloved, multi-language humanity surrounds you.

Craig and I signed up for ski lessons as a way to explore the vast ski area. Our ski instructor leads us on all the *pistes* (hills/runs) that have even a smattering of snow. A majority of the runs remain closed due to lack of snow and hazardous rocks. His instructions in English, "Float down the hill, carefully." He's great fun. Half way down the hill, we stop at a very out-of-the way log cabin, obviously a local hangout or a haven for lost skiers. After too many beers, we are expected to make our way back to the lodge, somehow the way back seems much longer than the exploratory run to the rustic cabin.

Leslie and the boys have a great time at the kids' facilities. Each night, we have to apprehend Leslie who is chasing around like a mad hyena after the other rag tag children left by their parents. Conner's in heaven with the giant buffets of food offered at every meal, while, Austin feels very powerful as the "best" (according to him) skier in his class. We opted to reserve the boys a room next to ours instead of bunking with them. Pre-teenage boys and malodorous ski gear are not a good combination. The housecleaner expressed her displeasure with them several times as she entered their room with a hanky tied over her nose. I'm not sure whether it's due to the un-flushed toilet or their personal "scent."

Finally snow falls, on the last two days of our stay at Alpe d'Huez. Although we experience skiing in some fresh powder, this complicates issues because we have to drive home in our minivan; the minivan is untested in snow conditions. The other two cars have four-wheel drive and most likely can handle the passes. The Ferrari of minivans proves to be our undoing.

Shannon, Crystal, and I leave the resort in the minivan with baby Kevin in the backseat. Shannon is the driver (for now) and I'm the navigator. I'm not a good navigator, but Shannon is tolerant of my direction dyslexia. Crystal has just finished a half-hour monologue of the intriguing plot of the movie, *The Others,* and we move on to the new kind of vegetable hair dye that's all the rage in France. Locals are easy to spot with their varying shades of crimson-colored hair. A most interesting topic, except when I next look up, Craig is gone, we have lost him at the *payage.*

We drive over four mountain passes and stop at the top of one while three hundred sheep pass by our minivan. We also stop once to relieve ourselves on the side of the road while baby Kevin waits in the car. Of course, this is also the only time a car comes around the corner. We haven't seen a car for at least one hundred miles. It's evening so perhaps he mistook us for an uncommon celestial phenomenon. I don't know.

• • •

Craig's Observations on the Ski Trip

We took a ski trip to the French Alps after Christmas. It was a simple plan: drive six hours IN DAYLIGHT, making reasonable allowances for stops for potty, meals, and petrol. As navigator and lead driver for the group of three automobiles, the pressure was on me to get us to Alpe d'Huez before darkness set in, when all would be lost (play *Gilligan's Island* theme song). The schedule was immediately compromised when the group elected to stop three miles from the house at McDonald's for the second breakfast of the morning.

I calmly did the math in my head and knew we could make up the lost time by increasing the speed on the autobahn from 130kph to 140kph, only 10kph over the speed limit. Just thirty minutes into the high-speed car rally across France, the unnamed occupants (Shawn's parents) in the last car caravan threw a fit and demanded a coffee/potty stop. Apparently, I had underestimated the required potty stop frequency—my original calculations incorporated the bathroom habits of camels, and I was traveling with a group of poodles in a forest of fire hydrants. Now we would travel at 150 kph (93 kph) for the remainder of the trip, to arrive before dark, a difficult task in a minivan in a windstorm.

It wasn't long before the coffee/potty stop schedule was completely compromised, and it was my fault; I forgot to factor in snack stops whereby certain occupants in the last car demanded to pull over for such essential road food as Cheetos and Snickers "melts on the seat of your pants, not in your mouth." They wouldn't be getting their damage deposit back on their rental car. Their tan "road pants" with brown and orange stains mysteriously disappeared at the end of the day. The brown stains were in a most unfortunate location on the pants, subjecting them to horrified stares at all subsequent stops. After many more stops, we somehow arrived at the ski village in complete darkness.

There was only one incident during the ski week with respect to language, and it was very minor. After a day of skiing, we decided to have a beer at the bar. Shawn, ever the Great Communicator, was peckish and ordered a snack. She thought she said to the handsome waiter in her best French, "Can I have a snack from the bar?" Correct translation was "Can I taste you?" This greatly increased the level of attentiveness by the male waiters. Normally, you would have to discharge a firearm into the ceiling to get table service, but after Shawn's request, we were waited on with stunning frequency by a wide variety of men. The general complaint about the lack of service in French establishments is simply not true.

Wherever we go in Europe, I've tried to be a good ambassador for the United States. In the gondola, I struck up an animated conversation with a Japanese man about Ichiro Suzuki, Seattl Mariner's All-Star right fielder. I offered my opinion that Ichiro was the best baseball player in the world. I thought he was going to cry with joy.

Unfortunately, I completely negated this act of goodwill when later in the day I accidentally hit a Belgian man in the head with a large rock. I was trying to be a good guy and throw a rock off the ski trail. As I tossed it behind me, this poor fellow skied up into a collision course with the rock. Time stood still as the rock arched towards his head. I tried to yell a warning, but only a squeak came from my throat. Lucky for him and me, it was only a glancing blow. A beer at the end of day remedied all bad feelings. I did the right thing in adopting a U.K. accent for the day, but he kept looking at me funny when I called him "mate." I think the mate thing is Australian.

After five months in the country, we had our first bad meal in France. The restaurant bragged about the "hot rock" grill, some sort of French version of BBQ. When we were seated, the grill was on the table and consisted of a can of Sterno heating a flat slab of granite. Mounds of raw sliced chicken, pork, and beef were brought to the table. The sight of meats bubbling in front of you was more than I wanted to see, particularly pork cooking next to the other meats. This didn't concern some of the more sanitary-challenged people at the table, but my sister is a microbiologist for the FDA, and her food stories have always scared the Hell out of me. I became a vegetarian for the evening. I don't believe the French "BBQ" would be a big hit in the USA.

• • •

There Are No Orthodontists in the Maldives

The kids really enjoyed Alpe d'Huez at Christmas time, and so feeling absolutely zero guilt we abandoned (their words, not mine) the kids, and traveled a fair distance for an adults-only scuba vacation in the Maldives. My parents accompanied us along with Shannon and Rick.

The Maldives are exactly eleven hand-wipes away (The flight attendants hand out cold, refreshing mini washcloths when they feel you've reached your limit, traveled long enough, or look as though you've accumulated some grime). Eleven hours and three plane rides later we arrived at the resort on one of the many Maldivian Islands, two-hundred miles south of the southern tip of India in the Indian Ocean.

The Maldivians are 100% Sunni Muslim and, thus far, the most engaging people I've met on this planet. According to the hotel manager, Americans rarely travel to this part of the world. The hotel staff is very curious to meet us, and find any excuse to talk to us. I can't help but notice the remarkable complexions and perfect pearly white teeth of each and every new staff member I meet.

They all have very straight, very white teeth, a good advertisement for an orthodontist . . . except there isn't an orthodontist on this particular small island. I asked. "We don't have an orthodontist here, maybe there is one in the capital city of Male, but, I don't think so," said the waiter. The resort encompasses the entire island; I have ambitions of jogging around the island, but being so close to the equator significantly stifles any rambunctious activity.

The spa at the resort is unique in the treatments they offer. During my "tension release" treatment, relaxation is just setting in, when suddenly, inexplicably, "whap, whap, whap" a banana peel or something slaps against the top of my head. Not wanting to offend the masseuse and not knowing the Male spa traditions, I remain mute. Now, (un-relaxed) I look wide-eyed at the floor, her feet leave the floor. I feel a growing pressure on my back and think: *My God, she is walking on my back! Should I say anything or just endure?* Again, not wanting to offend these kind people, I endure and live to tell about it. One can't be too careful with a Maldivian masseuse.

The six of us signed up for The Open-Water Scuba Certification course, an intensive dive course that lasts most of the week. Our two instructors are of German descent, and either don't get our jokes, have no sense of humor, or take the course work entirely too seriously. It's one thing to be safe under the water and practice new procedures, but entirely another to actually complete an entire book of assignments while on vacation. By the end of the week, the dive-master cracked a smile, but only once.

The entire island is one inch above sea level. Corals protect the island from Tsunamis, so the island doesn't suffer the same devastation as other Tsunami prone areas where coral reefs have been destroyed. The coral reef is teeming with sharks, barracudas, parrotfish, eels, and massive groupers just to name a few, not a usual sight on a dive vacation. Perhaps because we're so isolated here in the Maldives, the sea life is still abundant. The coral reefs exude all colors of the rainbow, definitely an unusual sight in the Caribbean, Mexico, and even South Polynesia, and other spots Craig and I have visited. The over-fishing and worldwide global warming of the seas have forever changed the natural beauty of the corals. Most of the time, we witness coral destruction with colors being brown, grey or slightly tangerine tinted coral.

On one particular dive, I seriously questioned my sanity when I followed the dive-master on a sketchy dive. As the dive-master jumps in the rolling seas to "test the current," she's carried away. The boat (the six of us are still onboard) follows her. She breathlessly climbs aboard, and says, "The current is a bit swift, I need to tie the line to a rock on the bottom." She then jumps back in the water, but only after adding a few more kilos to her weight belt. Somehow, she descends to about thirty feet and ties the sturdy line to a rock. She then pops to the surface after about five minutes, and says, "Hold the line and jump in, don't let go of the line." Holding the line assures that the current to the stern of the boat won't carry us away to where the stuttering motor is sure to make mincemeat of the unfortunate diver.

I realize I'm not only a lemming, but also an idiot. I jump in and begin to descend with much trepidation. Fish race past me, as if on an underwater treadmill. I immediately fill my wetsuit with liquid as I try to turn around and look for Craig. Large mistake, my mask is almost ripped off by the current. At the end of the life-saving line, I must somehow let loose my iron grip on the rope and free swim to the inviting-looking, currentless gulley ten feet further. This seems an impossible task as I fruitlessly swim in place, making no progress until I feel a giant surge behind me. Craig treading water behind me pushes my tank down to help me navigate the current. This helps, but as I look at my gage, I realize the dive is nearly over because I used up half my air swimming to the bottom. Our dive profile consists of swimming around the gulley and then hauling ourselves back up the line. Again, Craig pushes me aboard like a spent whale, where I lay on the bottom of the boat encumbered by my gear. I'm too tired to take it off. I'm so unnerved that I rant for a few minutes to the smiling Maldivian driving the boat; he assumes I'm insane and ignores me. I skip the next dive due to frayed nerves. I have about one nerve-wracking dive every three years or so, at which point I then rant about it for the next two or three years.

Despite this auspicious end to our vacation, we truly enjoyed our time with the Maldivian people and the lack of lines we usually encounter at the resorts while traveling with the kids.

The kids are more than happy to see us upon our return home; nothing is broken (always a worry in our art-laden rental home). Shannon reports that all of her children are recovering from the stomach flu, and pretends to be sorry she wasn't there for her little darlings.

It's rather depressing to return home to the unfriendly faces of the French, the complete opposite of the Maldivians. Sigh. It's surprisingly chilly, and the bumpy cobbled roads remain slippery, putting an end to our bike riding for now. Ready for a different sporting adventure, Craig and I decide to check out the tennis clubs in the area.

• • •

Craig's Observations on the Euro and the Malidves

On January 1, we were privileged to experience the conversion of Francs to Euros. With the Euro valued at 90% of the U.S. Dollar, the conversion was easy for me, 1€=USD. For the French it was a little more difficult. Imagine if the dollar was replaced with the "Amero" tomorrow, and it was worth 6.5 dollars. It wasn't easy for the poor French, but I must say the conversion was seamless and by the end of the first week, merchants clearly preferred the Euro currency rather than Francs for cash transactions. Maybe it's time for Mexico, Canada, and the U.S. to consider a common currency, so I can purchase a *cerveza* in Cabo without the unnecessary stress of math problems on vacation.

After New Year's, we traveled to the Maldives, a chain of tiny islands off the southern tip of India. This is Europe's version of Hawaii with no roads, cars, and locals who are actually happy to see you. The scuba diving was superb. On one dive, I stopped counting sharks after about thirty.

After a week of living with the most helpful people in the world, it was culture shock to arrive back in France. At the airport rental car desk in Nice, with a pre-paid reservation for a nice sporty car, I was told, after forty-five minutes of standing at the counter, that my car was not available. "No problem," I said, still in relaxed vacation mode and hoping for an upgrade to the next level of automobile. A single upgrade was not possible; the only vehicle available was a double upgrade. The counter person was upset when I didn't agree to return the upgraded car the next day for the original car we reserved. I explained that our house was one hour away and I was simply too busy to take two hours out of my day to return the car. The counter person relented with a big frown on her face. With a big smile, I signed the papers and hopped on the bus to the distant car lot to pick up what I was sure would be a Porsche or BMW. My expectations were unrealistic. A double upgrade in France is a pizza delivery van driven previously by a chain smoker.

～ Part V ～

Joining the Local Clubs

Le Vignal Tennis Club

In January, Craig and I joined Le Vignal, the local tennis club. We also signed up Rick and Shannon, figuring we could play with them if we're unsuccessful at making any friends. However, I have high hopes that we may latch onto some friends because the tennis club is run by an Englishwomen. As we tour the club and the clay courts, I can actually understand the language. What a bonus! We've stumbled upon a small ex-pat community, only five minutes from our home.

Le Vignal is off the beaten path, actually down a dirt road leading to the rather shabby, run-down club. The French are serious about their football (soccer) and their tennis, but the French are known for their love of good, fresh food. The unremarkable club entrance belies the existence of a small, but noteworthy restaurant that serves delectable lunches and dinners.

Le Vignal is also notable for its clay tennis courts. Everyone over thirty should play on clay tennis courts. The surface allows even the most arthritic player freedom to dash from side to side without suffering the ill effects of the hard-pounding surface we have in the United States.

Craig and I take tennis lessons from Philleeep (Philipe), a Frenchman and "the tennis Nazi." Philipe is rather stern, and he rarely cracks a smile. The one-hour lesson drags on with each "Americanized" comment he makes. "Home-run Mariners" is one of his favorites, but I'm usually too knackered to laugh. My old nemesis, "fat foot," a medical condition called *lymphadema* causes me a lot of grief during the lessons, so much so that I bring a cooler with an icepack for my ham-sized foot. I simply immerse my foot in the frigid water after practice. Philipe is immune to my whining and sniveling as I down Advil like vitamins. Sadly, my right arm is also lame from my inability to perfect the "correct" forehand stroke.

My tired old arm lost it perkiness after the first few lessons, as I continued to make mistake after mistake. Until I'm able to perfect the forehand stroke with correct "topspin," I'm doomed to forehand Hell. "Oh, come on, Shawn," Philipe says in a disdainful manner or "Let's go Shawn." Philipe points out a particularly apt pupil of his who's playing immediately next to us. He extols the beauty of her swing and the quickness of her feet. He then says, "She isn't bad." "Not bad" is the epitome of a French compliment. "Show me!" he shouts with such command I'm afraid to do otherwise. Apparently the "swat" technique I use is no longer in vogue, and Craig piles so many balls against the net, it looks as though he's using the net as his partner. But for now, I'm mindful that I'm lucky to be playing tennis in the brilliant sunshine with Philipe, the Nazi tennis coach.

Tomorrow I begin French/English conversation group at the library with Shannon, hopefully an improvement over French class.

La Bibliothèque

Shannon persuades me to join the French/English conversation class at the local library. She says all of the members have been asking about me since the Christmas party. I can only reason that they must really be frantic for English speakers. Rick refuses to attend, reasoning that his verb conjugation isn't yet perfected. I usually speak in "first person," hence, the cave man French I often refer to. "Me want two baguette." What could be clearer?

During my first class, I sit next to a man with a lisp, or maybe he has food in his mouth. He's my "conversation partner." I don't understand a word he says or the language he's using. We don't progress beyond introductions.

At the following class, I'm one of three English-speaking students in my group of eight adult peers. I turned in my paper entirely written in French on the subject of "Why clubs and societies are important to me". What the Hell kind of topic is this for a first-time student? One of the French-speaking students corrects my paper. The marks on my paper confirm my dismal knowledge of the French language. My paper is filled with red pen slashes. To make matters worse, the entire class reviews my paper and makes suggestions. *"Tu comprends?"* (You understand?) You American fool, of course this isn't what they said, but I'm sure they were thinking it. While writing my paper, I spelled words phonetically in order to pronounce the language correctly, assuming I'll have to read my paper to the class. I didn't know that another student would be reading my paper or I would have spelled words correctly. My downfall is complete when I discover two of my fellow students are teachers. In the end, "good effort" seems high praise indeed, maybe on the level of "not bad," a common French compliment.

When we finished correcting papers, we practiced oral French/English conversation. The French women next to me, happily discusses a new "cock" that moved to her neighborhood. *What the heck? I'm definitely living in the wrong neighborhood, who knew the French were so risqué?* I wonder if there's some sort of undercover wife-swap thing going on in the outskirts of Grasse. This is especially surprising because the library group consists of men and women in their sixties. The cock-talk-woman extols about the beauty of the cock's feathers and his lovely early morning crowing. I'm completely at loss about how to relay in the French language the significance of her use of a double entendre. Even Craig would have problems explaining her *faux pas* with his hand signals.

Conner and Leslie seem to have no problems with language *faux pas* when they play with the gang of neighborhood children who congregate on a regular basis in our large olive orchard.

Leslie won the trifecta in friends when the triplets (two girls and a boy) moved next door. At dinner, Leslie explains they (the triplets) are from England and attend the coveted Mougins School. She has no other information for me, thus giving me a perfect excuse to drop in next door (though not visible from our home) and introduce myself. Certainly, knowledge of your child's whereabouts must be a common thing among French/English/American cultures, and of course it's fortunate she speaks English.

The next day, Leslie and I hike across the olive orchard and climb over the stone wall to the house of the triplets. The house is extremely rustic but charming and it appears the owners are in the midst of a rather ambitious construction project. Perhaps this is the reason for our spotty water supply however I determine not to mention this on our first meeting.

The front door is nearly impossible to see due to the massive tree, which sits in front of the door. It's been cut into three pieces as though it's some sort of kindling for giants. "Hello? Hello? Is anyone home?" I said as I pushed the heavy door open. "Down here, in the basement," said a chirpy voice. I continue to talk as we walk down the stairs and into a dormitory style room. "Hi, I'm Leslie's mom from next door, just wanted to introduce myself."

A perfectly coifed blond woman walks towards me and extends her hand. Of course, she exclaims about the mess and the construction and then there's the firewood in front of the door. Firewood? She must be joking, it would take someone months to cut up the so-called wood, and why wasn't the wood delivered in pieces that could actually fit in a fireplace. However, this discussion never takes place because she then says she simply must get the sheets pressed before the beds can be made. "I just can't put my children to bed in rumpled sheets," she said and seeing my puzzled look, "Well, don't you press sheets in America?" "Ahhh, no we don't, at least I don't," I said. She shakes her head and continues with a slave-like devotion to iron the sheets.

Somehow, I feel as though we've gotten off to a bad start, with me being a non-sheet-presser and therefore a neglectful parent, I don't see how I can redeem myself. I make my excuses while offering to take the triplets for the afternoon. Maybe kid-sitting would soften her up, it's not like I have a lot of friends in the neighborhood. "That would be lovely, I'll see you at half past then, shall I?" Feeling like an absolute hillbilly, I respond in kind and leave her to the sheet pressing as the children trail along behind me.

The following week, I have another opportunity to meet a neighbor, this time through Conner. Thank God for the kids or I'd have no friends—not that the coifed English women next door has become a bosom buddy of mine—yet.

The Swim Club

"Mom, can I join the swim team, Alex across the street is on the swim team and his dad says I can join the team." This said while hopping from foot to foot with a few sporadic claps. Conner is often full of half-truths and stories he wishes were true so I don't take him too seriously. "No problem Conner, but I'll need to talk to Alex's dad," I said. "He's at the bottom of the driveway waiting for me in the car," Conner told me. This scenario is typical of my impulsive son however I want a bit more information before I send him off with a stranger.

Once Conner gathered up his speed suit, goggles, and towel, we hopped in the car and raced down the driveway. After all the man was in a hurry and to walk down the driveway would have taken fifteen minutes. The neighbor from across the street leaps out of his car upon seeing us and forcefully shakes my hand as well as Conner's. *"Êtes-vous bien?"* (You are well?) He said, *"Oui, bien."* (Yes, well.) Having just witnessed my son's first French conversation, although a bit limited, I'm momentarily silent.

The neighbor asks in very halting English if I speak French. I reply with my standard phrase. *"Oui, un* bit, *vous parlez lentement."* (Yes, a bit, you speak slowly.) It turns out our neighbor is the coach of the swim team and is willing to drive Conner three times a week to the swim club in Grasse. Certainly this would be nice but I'm still rather unsure. I haven't seen the swim club, have no idea where it is or when Conner will return. I speak a few awkward phrases and then pantomime the rest. In this case, sign language worked admirably well because I don't know the words for "I will follow you in my own car." Conner rolls his eyes but doesn't seem too surprised by the idea of his overprotective mother trailing behind in her own minivan.

There are no parents at the pool, most likely because there are no chairs or bleachers to sit on. The other swim coach tells me in no uncertain terms that parents are not allowed on the pool deck. I can wait outside if I want—all said in English. Somewhat embarrassed, I slink outside to sit in the car for an hour.

"Did you make the team? How was it?" I ask, as Conner gets into the car. "Of course I made the team," says my very self- assured son, "but the coach does a lot of yelling. What, I don't like that, maybe this isn't such a good idea." Conner assures me he doesn't care about the yelling and his French teacher shouts at him at school so it's no big deal. This gives me pause for thought, are parents not allowed in activities so the coaches and teachers have free reign to exercise their tonsils? Seeing Conner is rather blasé with the conversation, I let it go. For now, he has made a new friend and is participating in his favorite activity. Sports cross the language barrier again.

The Local Gym

I've combed the Internet and the Yellow Pages and located an athletic club. It's approximately five miles away. After convincing Craig we really need to join the athletic club, he agrees to accompany me to look it over.

Even though it's only five miles away, it takes us a half an hour to get there.

Driving in the countryside in France necessitates many circuitous routes. I can't think of one place I drive to daily that I don't have to drive up a one-way street (the wrong way), and then go through eight or ten roundabouts. On the back roads, people think nothing of stopping to chat (while sitting in their cars with the motors running). I've waited ten or fifteen minutes behind three cars while the drivers of two stopped cars hang out their windows and discuss the new fence or whatever it is they talk about. Strangely enough, no one honks or yells. They just turn off their cars and wait. So different from the pushing and shoving non-conforming lines the French seem to love. The freeway is the exception; one takes their life in their hands when driving the excessive speed limit. The *payage* (toll) stops usually result in some sort of mishap leaving me completely drenched with sweat before my destination. Suffice it to say, driving anywhere usually takes more time than expected.

The athletic club is filled with wall to wall people—no English spoken. I manage to convey that we would like a pass for a month. Apparently my terminology worked because she handed us two slips of paper and waved us away, no tour included.

Free weights and weight machines don't need any language interpretation. Fitness is the language here unless I want to take the step class. Somehow, I don't think I can follow the step class leader by sight while listening to incomprehensible rapid-fire French instructions.

Usually I'm in my own little world at the club because I only catch about every fifth word spoken. However, today is a banner day—I recognized an English voice, and I made a beeline for the owner of the voice. It's Max's mom and dad, having previously met them at the International School. I strike up a school-related conversation with them. She grew up in Grasse and speaks perfect English and French. She is a font of information, and knows the best shortcuts, hairdressers, and doctors. He's currently working in the country for an American company. We arranged playdates for the kids and parents and left feeling very pleased we can add two more acquaintances to our small group of friends. I believe Shannon and Rick are still in the lead because they have younger children. Everyone knows parents of younger children hang around the school more, thus making it more likely to develop friendships. Of course, my sister won't admit to this supposition of mine, she's still laughing about the last "friend" I made at the International School.

Dinner With 'The Jacket'

Craig and I vaguely know the mother of Leslie's friend, Ginger. She's an English woman who lives in the nearby town of Valbonne. We met through our eight-year-old daughters who play together at school.

Ginger's mother invited us over to dinner with her fiancé and a few other couples from the Valbonne area. We arrive in a thoroughly crabby mood because of my inability to read the map (French or otherwise) and poor directions from Ginger's mom.

The door is slowly opened by a "Lurch-like" (recall *The Addams Family*) grey-haired gentleman sporting velvet slippers and a Smoking Jacket! The last time I saw a smoking jacket was on Jimmy Stewart in *Rear Window*. We are apprised of "The Jacket's" background immediately, he is the eldest son of a long line of wealthy plantation owners in the deep-south. This all relayed in a very strange accent, "Ah'm the black sheep of the family, our people have a plantation in the South." Making matters worse, he is "in his cups." His accent is an affected mixture of upper-crust English accent and an unmistakable southern drawl.

Wondering where Ginger and her mom are, we're encouraged to make ourselves comfortable on the two-person sofa while The Jacket stumbles to the cocktail table. My daughter, Leslie, sensing all isn't right in this household, wisely scampers off to find Ginger. We gladly slurped down a few drinks thinking we're in for a long slog. As Craig and I gulped our drinks, we give each other "the look" that only long-married couples exchange. "Get me the heck out of here."

The Jacket is eager to show us his musical knowledge of Northwest musicians, and turns up the volume to an ear-busting crescendo on his stereo. "Craaaag" (said with a short vowel sound), "you must know this band, come on Craaaag, who are they?" Craig is paralyzed into near hysteria as The Jacket plays his air guitar with great enthusiasm. Our host's face is a contorted Halloween mask, mouth drawn decidedly down one side. I excuse myself to the bathroom to recover my composure, leaving Craig playing with his own "air drumsticks."

When I return, Craig is now slumped into the two-person sofa with the bleary-eyed Jacket who sits perilously close to Craig as he (Jacket, not Craig) extols the virtues of Northwest bands.

Thirty minutes later, Ginger's blowsy-haired mother scurries into the room, *tsk-tsk*ing The Jacket for his impromptu performance. "What will they think of you, Ashley?" and "For Gawd's sake, Ashley, turn the music down."

We are now desperate to escape the madhouse, but the rest of the guests arrive, an assortment of British ex-pats, all clearly used to Ashley's preference for the air-guitar. They immediately repair to the dining table, and Craig and I follow.

We sit as far away from Ashley as possible, and prepare for a marathon meal while Ashley berates people's use of the Internet. Everyone at the table vehemently opposes Ashley's moronic ideas about the world-wide-web. However, Ashley sticks to his guns. "Ahhh only keep track of maaa business on paper."

Our hostess disappears again, and then rushes back into the room and literally throws a large plate of BBQ ribs on the table—and nothing else. Well, of course there is wine, lots of wine, until Jacket falls asleep an hour later, his head peacefully propped on his gnawed spare ribs.

I don't think Craig and I are good at picking friends over here.

Once home, Craig and I discuss the possibility of using the train to visit other towns. Our friend, Susan, regularly uses the train, saying it's surprisingly "stress-free," and although it's not always on time, it beats driving to visit distant towns.

Menton Lemon Festival

The lemon is the symbol of the small town of Menton. Deeply rooted and celebrated since 1895, the parade of lemon floats is a "must see" for tourists traveling to the Côte d'Azur. The climate in Menton is temperate and perfect growing ground for the celebrated fruit. The lemon festival or *fête* has become a very popular town *event.*

Menton, France, is a small town on the Riviera, some 50 kilometers north of Cannes. The weather in Menton is pleasant; they have none of the nasty mistrals we occasionally experience in Grasse. A lemon lover's paradise, Menton embraces lemons; lemon trees grow at every corner. Colorfully dressed vendors sell lemonade and Limóncello, a lemon liquor. Because Menton has a big festival and parking is limited, Rick, Shannon, the kids, and I decided to take the train as our friends advised. Shannon's nanny, Crystal, decided to drive and join us later.

Our train arrives close to departure time but, makes many stops on the way to Menton, the proverbial "milk run."

As we watched the parade of Pinocchio, dogs, birds, lemon trees, and assorted other floats circle the small town of Menton five times, we wondered aloud how Crystal would fare on the two-lane road from Nice to Menton, and much later we hear her strange but true story.

Crystal's Story

Crystal says, when she arrived in Menton, she drove around the town at least five times looking for a parking place. (This is one of the reasons we took the train.) As she waited at a stop sign, suddenly, an old lady with a lemon print scarf pounded on her window, scaring her to death. The old women jabbered at her while pointing at an equally old fellow shuffling across the road. Of course, Crystal doesn't understand a word the old woman says. (Although Crystal somehow understands every word that two-year old Kevin says.) She (old lady) scoffed at her, and then waved the hunched-over geezer to her car. He slowly made his way to the car, and she shoved him into the auto and got in herself. Crystal said she was sure there was more scolding but of course she couldn't understand, but the old women's tone said it all. Crystal followed the woman's crooked finger and drove forward.

Being optimistic, Crystal thought they must want her to drive them to their parking place. She assumed the old people would then shuffle slowly out of her car and, move their car and Crystal would get the coveted spot. She happily drove them, and tried not to listen to the old guy. "You do not speak French." He said. He held up a long arthritic finger, and pointed in a direction, she immediately followed his well-weathered finger, she doesn't speak French but she can read "International Sign language!"

She drove about a half a mile at which point he said, *"Arrêt,"* or stop. She understood that much and was thrilled because she had a parking place. Maybe it was worth listening to the old people jabber and shout at each other and at her.

They laboriously climbed out of the car with a *"merci,"* and walked into a café. Hold on, thought Crystal, where is my parking space? Of course she couldn't say this out loud because she still doesn't speak French. Crystal was flabbergasted; she couldn't imagine two old geezers hitchhiking in the United States.

∼ *Part V* ∼

Travelogue
in and out
of the Country

Egypt

The International School of Nice has another week-long break from school. Craig and I wonder aloud if we should go anywhere or stay home and explore the countryside. "Why don't we visit Egypt?" asks Conner. He studied Egypt in school last year and is fascinated with ideas of mummies and tombs. Booking a trip to Egypt isn't a problem at this late date because Americans remain hesitant to travel since the terrorist attack on September 11and let's face it, who wouldn't prefer traveling to Egypt as opposed to driving through the countryside with three argumentative kids. No contest.

We selected the Abercrombie and Kent (A & K) travel agency, because we used them on our trip to the Maldives, and traveling with them is seamless. The tour includes several days "on land" at each end of the seven-day trip and four days on a small cruise ship on the River Nile.

The A & K tour guide greets us at the Cairo airport. Our smiling guide is quite recognizable in his crisp white shirt, tie, and badge with the A & K logo. This is a huge relief because the Cairo airport is a sea of people. Our small, pale-faced family swims upstream amidst mass confusion. Having a guide also relieves Craig and me from our usual travel bickering, which ensues regardless of where we travel. "I thought you brought the directions to the hotel?" "No, you said you put them in your wallet." Luckily, we have the guide, who takes care of every little detail.

The guide, Mohammed, escorts us to a waiting van where I thankfully accept a bottle of water from a very friendly local. Only later when we drive out of the airport do I realize my mistake as I witness the now not so friendly fellow running after our van, his long robes flapping about his legs. I mistakenly stiffed him out of his money for my water. The poor fellow breaks a sweat chasing the van; he manages to catch us in the garage, and angrily bangs on the door. Mohammed is surprised. I said weakly, "I didn't realize I was supposed to pay for the water, I thought he was your assistant." Mohammed quickly hands the panting fellow his money, at which point we learn our first lesson, the vendors are VERY persistent and nothing is FREE.

While still in Cairo, we visit the Egyptian museum where we see mummies, sarcophagi, and King Tut's treasures. The mummies are four thousand years old and still have their teeth, hair, and skin. Our Cairo tour guide is extremely thorough, so much so that we beg for a break after three hours.

Later in the day, Austin, Leslie, and I crawled through the hobbit-hole entrance of a pyramid and down a long, increasingly taller hallway to the center of the pyramid. Austin and I walked hunched over for some time until the tunnel opened up to reveal a giant treasure and burial chamber, devoid of treasure. Of course most of the existing Egyptian tombs have been robbed, but standing inside the pyramid is a surreal experience, imagining what it took to build this great structure. Our guide believes many more tombs remain buried under the existing dilapidated shacks where the locals now live. Under Egyptian law, an Egyptian resident must report any "found" treasure on the property; however, "discovered" treasures allow the locals to maintain a lifestyle just above the poverty level.

On the same day, we visited the Sphinx or "stinks" as pronounced by Leslie. Craig snaps yet another posed picture of the four of us in front of the Sphinx. Our tempers grow shorter with each ensuing photo in front of a "picture-worthy" structure. I offered to take some action shots, but Craig says all of my action shots are blurry. Perhaps he's right, but at least they're interesting.

Everyone is exhausted, and I'm wishing for a nap by the hotel pool however, the guide has another treat in store for us. "Would you like to go on a camel ride?" I'm about to gracefully decline the offer when Austin perks up with a chirpy, "yes."

Perhaps all tourists hitch a ride on a dromedary. Frankly, this doesn't appeal to me at all, but I'm a good sport. The camels know the path through the streets and take a "scenic" route bypassing the dump. I'm terribly worried the camel in front of me (Conner's camel) is going to suddenly turn around and bite my leg; his teeth look rather nasty. Luckily, his camel is satisfied with bumping along the street. Again, my imagination works overtime, as I'm precariously perched atop the giant beast. *What if these hump-backed creatures buck like horses?* I think to myself. Fortunately, my camel is well-behaved and I survived the ride with no mishap. The kids likened the camel ride to "a pony ride," they are nonplussed about the entire experience.

Our first stop today is a carpet factory, where the average age of a worker is twelve. Perhaps sensing the kids' unenthusiastic response about a possible "shopping experience," the enterprising guide entices the children with tales of flying carpets.

My oldest son is thirteen, and I feel very sorry for the little waifs who work industriously on the giant looms. Our guide assures us that the local children are fortunate to have this job. After working the morning shift they attend school at the factory, where they have the privilege of learning to read and write. The earnings the kids bring home from their morning shift helps put food on the table. Hopefully, this puts things in perspective for my children. Pulling weeds for an hour in our yard shouldn't be viewed as hard labor.

My sympathy sensors are still on high as we tour the carpet factory. Craig recognizes this, and starts to push me towards the door but not before a beautiful rug catches my eye. I whisper to Craig, "I wonder if the kids working here wove this very rug?" Craig pulls harder on my arm as the proprietor drapes the carpet in front of me. Craig and I compromised; the factory owner will stop by the hotel when we return from our cruise down the Nile to negotiate a "rock-bottom deal" for us. This leaves Craig and me plenty of time to discuss our "rock-bottom" price.

Today, our first stop in Cairo is the famous Mosque of Muhammed Ali also called the Alabaster Mosque. It is a popular tourist destination and clearly visible perched atop a hill in Cairo. Visitors are welcome as long as they are respectfully dressed and remove their shoes. The Mosque is stunning with numerous stained glass windows and arched ceilings. Muhammed Ali was one of the great governors of Egypt in the modern age and he had the Mosque commissioned in the 19th century.

Crouched and sitting, the local people of Cairo pray in the Mosque while we listen in rapt attention to Mohammed's (coincidentally our guide's name) explanation of the pilgrimage to Mecca. Prayer takes place five times a day for a follower of Islam. Mohammed, our guide, is a devout Muslim and explains the Five Pillars of Islam that a Muslim must follow in order to make it to paradise. All five laws are followed religiously and accepted as a matter of course (at least by our guide Mohammed), such as, "There is no true God except Allah and Muhammed is the messenger of God." Mohammed is very enthusiastic about one law in particular.

A pilgrimage to Mecca is an event most Muslims strive to accomplish at least once in a lifetime. Because this requires traveling a long distance and taking time off from work, not everyone is able to attain this lofty goal. Mohammed himself hopes to make the pilgrimage the first half of the last month of the lunar year. He said his mother was sick last year and he couldn't go on the pilgrimage. It's clearly an event he is really looking forward to.

The believers of Allah are expected to complete the self-sacrificing journey to the Plains of Arafat, located in the valley of Mina. It is a journey of deprivation and spiritual renewal, requiring camping on the desert sands and strength of character to make the five-day hike. Once the pilgrimage is completed, the Muslims are known as Hajji, a well-recognized honor among their people.

If circumstances prevent followers from attending the ceremony while traveling, they must start the journey again the following year or when circumstances allow. The travel timing must be perfect because the actual ceremony only lasts one day.

Muslims pray five times a day. Later in the trip, we would hear their sing-song melody and the call for prayer often while floating down the Nile. The Muslim beliefs and traditions give us all pause for thought for the remainder of the afternoon, at which time our contemplations are put to an end with a treasure hunt for the kids in the busy bazaar of Cairo.

Mohammed has no apprehension for our blond-haired children running through the massive bazaar while looking for treasures. He offered Craig and me a drink in the local Hookah lounge while the kids scavenged the streets of Cairo . . . unchaperoned. We declined.

As Craig wandered the streets with the boys, and I trailed after Leslie, we discovered yet again a common bond all people of our small planet share, most people love small children. The locals wanted to take pictures of Leslie and engage her in conversation. This sudden popularity overwhelmed Leslie as she cowered by my leg, so I posed for picture after picture with Leslie. I'm sure the giggling schoolgirls didn't want me in the picture with cute little Leslie, but it's the best I could do for them.

After the kids' treasure hunt, we fly to Aswan where we meet the ship for our trip down the River Nile. The small ship is lovely, with large comfortable rooms, a blessing for Austin because he's sick. He somehow "forgot" parental and guide warnings and brushed his teeth with the tap water at the hotel in Cairo. The water bottles by the tap in the bathroom should have been a dead giveaway for him. He now pays the price with frequent trips to the restroom.

While on the boat, Leslie and Conner immediately form a gang of children who call themselves The Cheese Down Gang (C.D.G.). When asked about the significance of the name, Conner responds, "I don't know." Every night after dinner, we endure "choreographed" dances from the C.D.G. Conner fancies himself a dancer much to the dismay of his brother who calls him a "Sally boy" while laughing himself sick at his brother's dramatic choreography.

The ship stops at a new sight every day, at which point the passengers break into small groups and hop into a conveniently parked van, piloted by our guide. The first stop at The Valley of the Kings doesn't look like much from the above ground, however entering the first tomb is like taking a step back in time. The hieroglyphics and vivid dyes (240 B.C.) remain visible even now. This is even more remarkable because the hieroglyphics aren't enclosed by Plexiglas and so remain free of glare from the bare light bulbs propped up on rickety stands in the underground caverns. Seventy burial sites exist in this valley alone, eleven of which are open at all times.

American tourism is at an all-time low, most likely due to 9/11. An armed guard stands at the entryway of our vessel, and the tourist attractions in Egypt are well-protected. At no point do we feel threatened, except by the overly aggressive vendors.

The ratio of tourists to vendors is 1/10; hawkers descend upon us as we leave each tomb. This is really tiresome. When asked, our guide simply says, "Make no eye contact with the street salesman." To make eye contact is akin to saying, "Hello, may I see your wares?" I'm inclined to politely respond, "No, thank you," and naturally look at the vendor as I do so. However, making eye contact or responding is initiating a conversation. Communication takes many forms here; the best form of non-communication is to simply walk by people while looking at the ground, or at the passing sights. I'm growing weary of names like, "Missy, Chickie," and the ever popular, "Hey lady." One particularly astute vendor called me Claudia, as in "Schiffer," so I bought a scarf from him. He's the same vendor who shouted, "Hey, Rambo," to Craig.

Much to our amazement, the hawkers continued to follow us even as our boat departed. As we sit on the upper deck of the ship, our conversation is interrupted by "Hey, lady!" from the seas below. The hawkers rowed alongside us in their little boats filled with plastic-covered merchandise. As I curiously look over the side, I'm nearly hit in the head with a large plastic bundle tossed on the deck by the desperate hawker. Craig throws the bundle back over the side of the ship before I have a chance to peek at the bounty. Craig missed his mark or maybe not, and the package landed in the water and sank. A lot of fist waving and shouting ensues from the salesmen when the precious parcel disappears from sight.

Earlier in the day while touring a bazaar we all purchased *galabeys* from the vendors. A *galabey* is an ankle-length, lightweight type of caftan that most of the local men wear with light cotton pants or boxer shorts underneath, most men and women wear them in the city. Our guide helped Leslie and me bargain with a vendor for several of them and some bangles. The Egyptians like to bargain and are insulted if you don't partake in the wager for merchandise. After bargaining and on our way back to the ship, we spy Craig and the boys in a very small stall in the back of the bazaar. Craig looks desperate to escape. This amazes me because Craig's job as a commercial real-estate developer requires him to make deals with all sorts of people, however Old Toothless seems to be getting the best of Craig at the moment. A large pile of goods rests at Craig's feet as he continues to count out his pretty paper Egyptian pounds; smaller bills are "piasters," (one hundred piasters make one Egyptian pound.) Our guide rescues him while I take a picture of the scene, our only action shot thus far.

In the evening we attend a "Galabeys Party." Our guide and the cook cut a rug on the dime-sized dance floor, and I'm more than happy to join them when invited. I perfected the local form of dancing with little problem, probably due to the repetition of one step only.

The cruise ends after four days. None of us wants to leave the ship, even Austin is up and around after the ship's chef acted as Austin's nursemaid, cooking him special meals for his sensitive stomach. However, I'm looking forward to meeting the rug company owner back at the hotel. I'm not convinced of Craig's bargaining ability after witnessing his earlier fiasco in the bazaar, however I know I'm worthless at the game of bargaining. Of course, it would help if Craig actually wanted the rug.

Back at the hotel, Craig does manage to buy the rug with the astute help of our guide, however not before he acquired saddlebags of sweat under each arm while in the throes of bargaining.

In summary, the Egyptians are fun, lovely people. They live in run-down shacks and walk barefoot through the muddy streets, and yet, they are happy and so welcoming and warm to all visitors. They have pride in their country and their work; the popular tourist attractions are well-protected for the safety of the tourists. We met the Secretary of the U.S. Embassy consulate while on our travels, and confirmed that visitors can and should feel entirely safe (unless attacked by a camel).

Rising early the next morning, the guide is ready and waiting to drive us to the airport for our return trip to Nice, France. The service with A & K has been impeccable and hassle-free, a relief when traveling in a foreign country with kids. I shudder to think of the comparisons to the lice-ridden Super Fun Happy Resort.

Returning to Nice actually feels like home, we're all eager to get back to familiar territory and a vaguely recognizable language.

I'm the Official Translator

The intricacies of the French language continue to pose problems for me. Yesterday, Levio, the property caretaker showed Craig a bag of cat food. Craig says, "Levio waved his hand back and forth over a bag of cat food like a magician and muttered something I couldn't understand."

Query? Why does Levio communicate with Craig when he knows I'm the official translator for the family? Craig assumes that now he, Craig, must feed Pepito. He deduces that Levio must be going on vacation.

Levio and I cross paths later the same day, and I haltingly asked him if I'm supposed to feed the neighborhood cat, *"Je mange Pepito?"* Levio replies in a language that sounds like muffled cursing. From what I can deduce, Pepito is a wandering neighborhood cat that makes an appearance from time to time—depending upon what sort meal is being served. As far as I know, Levio doesn't even own the blasted cat.

Making no progress with my question about Pepito, I asked Levio if he would mind helping the neighbors cut up the giant tree posing as firewood. The neighbors, a young British couple with triplets live next door although we can't see their home from atop our mini mountain. Leslie and Conner met the triplets while playing outside in the olive orchard. Excited that they had new friends, I walked over and introduced myself to the triplets' parents. I wish I could explain this to Levio—but I dare not try. Levio, his friend, and I walk next door in not so companionable silence.

The so-called firewood is a large tree cut into three pieces, where it rests in their front yard blocking the entrance to the front door. Our new next-door neighbor suspects the firewood delivery people won't be returning to finish the job. Perhaps leaving a tree in the yard is a finished job here in France.

Our English neighbor says she's fluent in French and understood the local newspaper ad to read, "Cut firewood delivered to your home." The giant tree cut into three pieces won't fit into their small fireplace unless they remodel their house around a new lumberjack-sized fireplace. Levio and his friend agree to cut the giant lumber into kindling of some sort. I ascertain this because both men nod yes when I make a firm chopping gesture with my hand. Having achieved some sort of "gesture-speak," I again ask Levio about feeding Pepito.

I notice both Levio and his friend are staring at me with faces aghast. My neighbor, the Englishwomen says perhaps she misheard me, but she thinks I said, "I eat Pepito." It's true I don't know the word for "feed", so I used the word for "eat." A simple enough mistake anyone might make, from here on, I will use only hand gestures with Levio.

I wondered aloud to my neighbor, "Are you having a hard time communicating with Levio?"

"Yes, because he's speaking a combination of French and Italian, and I don't think he understands my English-accented French," she said. This makes me absurdly happy it's not just me who can't communicate with Levio.

French-Sized Kindling

Today, Levio and his friend brought a giant wood-cutting machine into our yard. Because Levio works for our landlord, I tried to explain to him that he must cut the neighbor's wood on his own time. Making hasty hand signals to signal him to stop chopping, and go back to his job on our grounds accomplishes nothing. Meanwhile, Craig witnesses this exchange while waiting for me in the car. He harps on me about my dangerous knowledge of French, and says I will get us all arrested if I'm not careful. I remind him that he doesn't have room to talk after he said Levio was going on vacation and I should feed the cat. In reality, Levio just wanted to show Craig the fine bag of cat food he bought the spoiled cat. A tense atmosphere pervades the car as we drive to the athletic club.

• • •

Craig's Observations on Levio and Pepito the Cat

Shawn's language skills have brought grief to the household again. Yesterday, the property guardian, Levio, spoke rapidly to me in French, holding a bag of cat food and gesturing towards the resident cat, Pepito. Pepito has it made; he lives in France and has two different sets of people looking after him, Levio on the weekdays and the neighbor lady, Mademoiselle Green Dress, on the weekends. He is fed both dry and canned food. If I'm reincarnated as an animal, I want Pepito's job. In any event, I understood Levio's communication perfectly without understanding a word of French: he asked me to feed the cat because he was taking the day off. Shawn, doubting my gift of non-verbal communication, marched down this morning to talk to Levio about Pepito. She thought she said, "I have fed the cat this morning," but unfortunately, her best French failed again and she said, "I ate the cat this morning." Levio, a sensitive animal lover, was seen roaming about the property, sobbing uncontrollably. Pepito has not made an appearance all morning and I'm concerned for Levio's well-being. He's presently on the highest spot on the roof, fixing something and I fear he may do something irrational if he doesn't see Pepito pretty soon. Reasoning that a French cat would have refined tastes for food like French people, I set out a plate of Brie cheese and fine crackers to lure Pepito into view. Pepito, waiting around the corner, immediately rushed over to the fine repast I prepared him and all is well again with Levio.

• • •

The Circus Finale

I don't know what it is about the French and these traveling circuses. The current circus in town is much the same as the last one except there's a performing camel and horse in addition to the always-popular dog. As you may recall, the last circus had only a dog and a goat. All of the kids enjoyed the new show except Austin who's now a teenager and deems these shows childish.

Leslie waxes on about the circus as I tuck her into bed that evening. She thinks that perhaps we as a family could start our own circus. I'm at a loss as to how to respond, because she is completely serious. She will be the star (what a surprise) and her cousin, Kylie, will be a mime, apparently a passionate career choice of Kylie's. My job is ticket taker and popcorn server, and her father will be the announcer. She doesn't have jobs for the other family members yet. She drifts off to sleep as dancing goats, camels, and dogs perform in her head.

I contemplate the life of a circus performer—perhaps I've missed my calling, because I've come to deduce that tennis may not be the sport for me, at least according to my progress thus far.

Tennis Torture

I learned to play the net today, a useful skill in tennis. I'd better be very proficient at the net because my left Achilles tendon is aching so badly due to daily sprinting drills that I can only hobble around the court. Standing at the net requires little sprinting. I'm limping along, and I have a game tomorrow with another club member, Stork, so named due to her long appendages. Philipe, my instructor says, "Stork isn't a good player and if you do not win, then, you should kill yourself." The French are very passionate about their sports, but this is a rather drastic statement. Maybe he is forgetting his English. I certainly hope so.

Craig is playing with a new partner also, a rather old fellow who certainly doesn't look tennis-worthy. Unfortunately for Craig, the old guy can place the ball exactly where he (old dude) wants it. For a minute, I imagined that Craig might throw his racket across the court, but he restrained himself at the last minute. I think my husband may be annoyed with my inadvertent instructions during a heated moment of the match, "Check your backhand grip." I noticed the look he shot me isn't the most loving.

• • •

Craig's Observations about Tennis

The first big tennis club tournament is coming up this weekend. We have entered the contest, under extreme duress from the club chairperson. I believe they needed a few pancakes to boost the egos of some of the other players in the early rounds. My tune-up match today was on center court, against my wishes. My opponent, an elderly French gentleman, was waiting for me. Looking him over, I thought, "sixty-something, grey hair, this won't take too long," and it didn't. He crushed me, 6-1; 6-0, in thirty-five minutes. For the life of me, I couldn't return a single backhand shot. Shawn sitting on the sidelines, made a helpful comment at the zenith of my frustration, "Honey, check your grip on the racquet." Luckily, I was on the far side of the court or I would have checked my grip around her neck. I can take no solace in his five-month lessons to my two months of instructions. My teacher, on an adjacent court, was not sympathetic.

In my lesson that followed the match, Philipe, my teacher, and a bald Frenchman, also showed no mercy. His English skills are perfect, but, he has limited his expressions during lessons to four phrases: "Come on, Craig; Let's go; Show me; That was out." Once he said, "Well done", but then caught himself and qualified the compliment. He has given Shawn several "very goods" in her lessons. I enjoy playing with him, as he can return virtually any shot I make, no matter how miraculous. Today's enjoyment was cut short, however, as it fittingly started to rain half way through the lesson.

• • •

Tennis Tournament

My opponent is the wife of Steffi Graff's tennis coach. Just the thought of playing her, no matter how vaguely she is associated with a professional tennis player, has me in a dither. The club personnel informed me of my partner's identity the day before, and I spent much of the evening worrying about the upcoming match. I reassured myself that just because her husband is an instructor doesn't mean she's a good player. It doesn't work.

Arriving early at the tennis club, I discovered that, like Craig, I've been assigned to the center court. Everyone in the restaurant will be witness to my spectacular success or miserable failure. No fewer than eleven people sit in my cheering section. When we are introduced, my new tennis partner is very stiff-lipped; perhaps, she's trying to intimidate me. It works. Stiff Lips has a wicked serve, but this doesn't dismay me as I'm used to playing with Austin, who relishes defeating me with his left-handed serve. My weakness is apparent after the first game. My legs immobile, I'm, what Philipe likes to call a statue, which translates to the same word in French. My one good shot aimed at her feet is perfect, but I'm so busy admiring my shot while maintaining my statue position that she manages to return it, of course, out of my reach. My cat-quick reflexes don't suffice. She returns my lobs with ease and, at one time, charges the net with a Tarzan-like yell that scares the living daylights out of me. I'm grateful I'm wearing light-colored shorts in case I embarrass myself further. Her one weakness is her aerobic capacity. She spends an inordinate time on the bench during breaks while trying to catch her breath. I look for the judge to call time, but he's talking to her husband, Steffi Graff's coach.

My sister hovers protectively by the fence as if she can somehow save me from further disgrace. At one point, she calls my opponents serve out which isn't exactly tennis etiquette, and she receives a stern look from the line judge. She's a good sister. At the end of the match, I apologize for my lack of skills and Stiff Lip nods in agreement. What kind of good sportsmanship is this? We shake hands and I walk slowly, shoulders slumped forward in defeat, to my cheering section. They greet me with comments such as; "You were able to return her serve" and "Your outfit was better."

I'm the proud owner of two additional bicycle wheels. This is French tennis terminology for 6-0, 6-0.

Conner played after me and makes it through two eliminations but failed on the third. Austin and Craig are first-time losers like me.

I return home to contemplate my loss when quite suddenly there is a shrill alarm sound.

Maison Fort Knox

The home security alarm system has a mind of its own. For the last several days the alarm goes off whenever it feels like it, usually every two hours or so—day and night. This makes for a most unrestful sleep. Craig is more sensitive to the blaring alarm than I am; "I'm moving to a hotel right now." It's the middle of night, so I reasonably reply, "I'm going back to sleep until it goes off again."

Everyone looks rather haggard the next morning. I send the kids off to school with bags under their eyes and look for Levio. Perhaps he can solve the mystery of the broken alarm.

Levio lets me have it with both barrels; this is very dismaying as Levio is usually impassive in his demeanor. I can only surmise it has something to do with Pepito, the cat, and my earlier language faux pas. Levio shakes the cat food bag back and forth while gesticulating madly and grumbling about my inability to feed or eat the cat. This is what I think he is saying, but I really have no idea. However I digress, I attempt to explain to Levio about the malfunctioning alarm. I think we have an understanding, mostly because I look like I have not slept in two days and the alarm goes off unbidden at that moment. Levio calls the "alarm society."

The "alarm society" says they will come in two days time; they actually do arrive in two days time and then say they don't work on this particular type of alarm. Craig threatens to go to the hotel . . . again.

Craig, now at the end of his rope, calls the homeowner in Norway who speaks to Levio. Things happen very quickly after the phone call. Levio takes off at full throttle in his little tin can car down the driveway to find someone from another alarm society to fix the buzzer.

I returned from the gym to find our house full of the alarm society employees. The intermittent blaring alarm problem takes the alarm society people two days to fix . . . nothing happens quickly here in France.

• • •

Craig's Observations on the Burglar Alarm

The burglar alarm is malfunctioning. Levio, still distressed over Pepito, called the owner in Oslo to report the problem and request new tenants for the house. If the cat doesn't return soon and the owner must make a choice between Levio and us, we'll be returning home to Seattle a little earlier than planned.

• • •

The Easter Bird

T
oday Leslie learned that the Easter Bunny doesn't exist here in France. The Easter BIRD leaves chocolate and other candies in slippers placed outside the front door for children to find on Easter morning. Because we have wild *sangliers* (pigs) and unattended dogs roaming our neighborhood, we opted to hide the slippered candy INSIDE our home.

On Easter Sunday, we enjoy a lovely brunch at Rick and Shannon's home until things turn chaotic during the traditional Easter egg hunt. My cousin, Kim, is visiting from Seattle for a month and her husband, Greg, will join us in a week. Her children, Madison and Dakota, respectively in third and first grade join in the Easter egg hunt. This makes for a rather large Easter egg hunt in Rick and Shannon's unfinished muddy yard. The men hide the eggs in the yard under rock shelves and in muddy holes while the kids shove and push each other while waiting at the locked front door. My own children trampled their small three-year old cousin, Kevin, although he didn't seem to mind as his mouth was full of chocolate.

After the outdoor mayhem, everyone appeared satisfied with their haul and peace reigned as eager mouths sucked on chocolate eggs.

The fourteen of us (three families) leave in two days time for a road trip to Avignon.

Avignon

A vignon is a destination I have fond memories of as a college exchange student. My sister's neighbors in the states offered their mother-in-law's rustic home, at a nominal rent, making it an easy decision to caravan to the middle of France.

On our six-hour journey to Avignon, Craig has some mishaps with the *payages* or tollbooths, as we know them in the United States. At one point, when the *payage* ticket machine eats his credit card, Craig presses the "Help" button and in a rather harried voice says to me; "What do I say?" Never good under pressure, I stammered some French phrase and let him fend for himself. The person at the other end of the speaker replied to Craig in a very strident voice, which does nothing for Craig's *payage*-anxiety. Craig, being a smooth representative for the United States, yells, "Hey, S**tbrick" back into the microphone in an equally harsh voice. Our son, Austin, laughs uncontrollably in the back seat, which isn't helpful. The atmosphere in the car is charged with tension. After this heated exchange, a smiling uniformed fellow emerges from the far away tollbooth station to take Craig's credit card—even though we're in the line for pre-paid customers. Craig quickly changes his demeanor to happy visitor but fools none of us.

It's dark when we finally arrive at our U-shaped *mas*, or farmhouse. According to Shannon, the farmhouse was built at the end of the nineteenth century. It's surrounded by other quaint stone houses in what I assume is a pastoral setting on the outskirts of Avignon. A lovely courtyard in the middle of the "U" is the perfect playground for the kids to run off their pent-up energy. The old house was built primarily as a summer residence, thus the heavy stone walls keep the house cool.

Entering our new temporary abode, we are pleasantly surprised with the "shabby chic" décor. That is, what we are able to see with the flashlights conveniently left at the front door. The fireplace in the kitchen has a giant iron kettle hanging over it. My pioneer spirit takes over as I think of making hot oatmeal in the morning for my usually crabby brood. But right now, the kids are whining and want to know where they're sleeping.

Craig and I select the bedroom over the kitchen on one side of the "U," while Rick and Shannon search for rooms on the other side. In the recesses of the antiquated old manse, we settle our boys in a small room with a double bed. They bitterly complain; "It's cold in here and I can see my breath." "Be quiet Conner and snuggle up with your brother. Here's a nice blanket," I say as I hand over what feels like a burlap sack. They both look at me with horror; pre-teen brothers don't like to cuddle. We leave them to their bickering and send Leslie off to sleep with her cousin, Kylie.

As luck would have it, the bedroom Craig and I picked is by far the largest bedroom in the house. Rick and Shannon wanted to keep an eye on their three small children and the master suite (our room) is very isolated.

Entering the master suite, Craig and I are pleasantly surprised by the large stack of firewood sitting by the fireplace. We have a blissful night's sleep under the warm comforter as the crackling fire heats the room. Rick and Shannon wake up three or four times in the night to tend to their sick children, not a good start to their day. Unbeknownst (we figured additional firewood was stacked beside the house) to us we use most of the week's supply of firewood that night.

The following morning, our boys are cuddled together and shivering under their one blanket. Because we searched for the bedrooms in very little light, we unknowingly put them to bed at the end of the "U" where they shivered uncontrollably most of the night. They groused in the morning about their accommodations and I felt a little sorry for them, but not enough to trade rooms.

When touring Avignon, we visited the Palais des Papes, or Palace of the Popes, a very austere palace because a lot of the furniture was lost due to fire.

Leaving the Palais des Papes, we entered the *place* or plaza where a show of sorts is taking place. A ghostly painted mime walked around entertaining the gathering crowd with strange contortions while his eyes mesmerized us with their glistening, fake, black painted teardrops. A tuxedo-dressed musician played his harp in the center of the place, he looks as strangely beautiful as his music. The rays of sun glistened off the musician's instrument while the kids rode round and round on the double-decker carousel.

During the afternoon, we walked to the Pont d'Avignon, the first bridge built for crossing the Rhône River. The bridge outside of Avignon was built in the eighteenth century, and only four arches remain of the original twenty-two, the remaining having been destroyed by the Rhône River during flood season. As we stood on the bridge posing for Craig's calculated picture in front of a recognizable scene, I remembered having a fellow classmate take the very same picture on this bridge when I was a student in Avignon. Yet another *déjà vu* experience from my long-past studious months here in Avignon.

The following day we visited St. Remy and Le Beaux. St. Remy is a little village about twenty kilometers outside of Avignon. It's surrounded by a fourteenth century stone wall, which encircles small tourist shops filled with the usual French trinkets. I grow weary of the miniature clay-baked provincial French husband and wife dolls sitting on the inevitable citron, rayon floral tablecloth (also for sale).

The kids and grown-up kids (husbands) adored Le Beaux a medieval village at the base of what is described in the brochure as a mountain, but what actually appears to be a giant rock. Climbing up the so-called mountain is a hike better suited for a mountain goat. The shale cascaded down on me as the children scampered to the top of the hill and hung precariously over the edges. There are no precautionary fences in evidence, and my stomach gives great lurches each time the kids scamper close to the edge of the cliff. I entice them down from the precarious situation with the lure of the medieval torture devices not yet tested.

The adults and kids are enamored with the torture devices and the catapults. Fortunately, we missed the "live performances" of over-zealous tourists attempting to fling themselves into the air. Instead, the kids inserted their heads and arms in the life-size wooden devices used to display the less fortunate who had committed a relatively innocuous crime.

During our car ride home we again encounter problems with the French *payage*. This time we can't escape a garage where we have foolishly parked our van. After we inserted the garage ticket in the booth, two floors above the exit (this in itself posed a problem), a mysterious voice from the intercom says it would be best if we report downstairs. Putting my face close to the machine I garble in French that *"Machine mangent billet et l'argent"* (machine eat ticket and money). The bodyless voice drones *état en bas* or report downstairs.

I approached the downstairs *payage*, as we have no choice. We can't exit the garage without a ticket. I'm confident in my French linguistic skills, having worked out my phrase in my head. I reasonably explain (in caveman French, present tense only) to the harried looking attendant at the "customer service" desk that we lost our money in the booth and didn't get a ticket or change for our twenty Euros. Craig remains in the car at the garage exit looking very irritated. The customer service attendant looks sideways at me, so I painstakingly explain again, throwing in a few extra pronouns for good measure.

I hear the minivan door slam but don't dare turn around. The ground begins to vibrate as Craig stomps over to the *payage*, I fear this isn't going to turn out well. I'm just making headway with my new friend when Craig interrupts us and says in a very loud voice with accompanying hand signals, "The machine ate our money and we want out of the garage right now!" I curse Craig in a low voice at which point he tells me, "A stern voice is the only thing this buffoon will understand." I resign myself to upcoming fisticuffs when another attendant emerges from a cubbyhole in the back and produces our change and our escape ticket. Craig smirks at me and stomps back to the car. I'm confident the tollbooth employee finally understood me and was just about to produce the ticket and change. Craig disagrees. Again, I find Austin hysterical in the backseat, while cousin, Kim, takes pictures of Craig thundering back to the car. This small exchange doesn't bode well for the long car trip back to Grasse.

My sister and brother-in-law are staying in Avignon for several more days. This worries me a bit because I now realize that Craig and I have used the entire stack of firewood each evening to warm our chilled bodies—leaving them no source of heat.

Once on the road and according to my cousin, Kim, "Craig took off like a bolt of lightning immediately after clearing the *payage*." I can attest to this as I watch Kim's visage fading behind us. Just because the speed limits are posted for Mario Anderetti-like drivers, doesn't require us to shoot down the freeway like a rocket. I say as much to Craig, but he's in the push-through zone, meaning nothing stops his progress. Poor Kim has only Austin as her navigator and I clearly remember his distractibility problem on my last trip with him to Florence.

When we finally arrive at Fort Knox, it's shut up tight and we have forgotten the key. Craig and I being both grumpy and tired blame each other for about five minutes and then realize we need to come up with a solution. We try all of the doors and shuttered windows. Luckily, cousin Kim left her French door on the bottom floor, unlocked for all burglars wishing to enter. After deactivating the alarm, we slowly tromp through the house; the master bedroom door is locked. The cursing begins again and I resign myself to sleeping on the couch. I'm just too tired to think of a solution for this problem. Thankfully, Craig is made of sterner stuff than I am, and he calls the landlord in Norway and locates the extra key in the master safe in the office.

• • •

Craig's Observations on Language

Let me ask you, after Shawn's various language mishaps in France, "I want a short haircut (horse ride)," "I ate (fed) the cat," "I love (you and your) watermelons," "Can I taste you?" do you really believe I would ask her how to say anything in French? Unfortunately, I was desperate. Finally, after seven months in the country, two situations arose within twenty-four hours where my tried-and-true method of communication, hand signaling, failed. It was impossible to communicate with hand gestures into a speaker box. As the cars stacked up behind us in line at the tollbooth, I had no choice but to ask Shawn how to say simple phrases in French. Lesson learned—in the future I will go to the *payage* booth staffed by a cranky French person instead of a person-less booth.

On the road trip to Avignon, we elected to travel via the autobahn, a toll freeway. At the last booth, I picked the shortest line of cars and found when it was my turn to pay there was an automated machine accepting credit cards. No problem, so far. Unfortunately, the credit card wasn't returned and the barrier gate didn't lift out of our path. I calmly pushed the help button and a rather crabby sounding Frenchman answered. I asked Shawn how to say in her second language, "My credit card is stuck in the machine." I carefully repeated Shawn's words into the speaker box. The ranting/screaming reply caught me off guard and I admit that I lost it for a few seconds. "Hey, S**tbrick" seemed like a reasonable and appropriate response to me at the time. No translation to French was required. I learned later that Shawn's words, correctly translated, were "I peed on my credit card and now it is stuck in the machine." This would explain the worker's coming out from the office with latex gloves on to remove the card and his keen interest in our license plate number.

The second tollbooth incident occurred not twenty-four hours later. In a parking garage in Avignon, we paid our parking bill at the automated machines. This time the machine ate the exit ticket and twenty Euros, failing to give us ten Euros in change. Somehow this was my fault, judging by the tone of the person's voice coming from the speakerphone. "Report downstairs to the office at once" was the unpleasant demand. I was loaded for bear now, but I let Shawn have first crack at the fool behind the bulletproof glass. I allowed her five minutes, before I could wait no longer. It was a good thing, as Mrs. Sucker American was reaching for her purse to pay twice. Seems her French failed her again. I skipped the hand signals and went straight to English, appropriately amplified, which they understood very clearly. The shakedown was shut down, an exit ticket and the correct change suddenly appeared, but somehow I came out of it the "Rude American." I later learned that Shawn thought she said, "I would like my ticket and change" to the attendant, but the correct translation was "I would like a massage and a car wash." She is borderline dangerous with her efforts to communicate.

For the foregoing sins, I have been banished to Seattle with the boys to work for ten days while Shawn and Leslie tour the best of Italy: The Riviera, Tuscany, and Lake Como. In the evenings, Shawn enjoys a glass of Chianti on the patio of a Five-star hotel served by an attentive, dark, and mysterious waiter named Julio, Antoine, or Alberto. I, on the other hand, enjoy the drive-thru service of local fast food establishments where the attentive cashier thoughtfully asks if I'd like "super size."

• • •

Shop 'Til You Drop

Kim, the girls, and I leave for Italy in a few days time, but until then we have a few days to shop and do some sightseeing in our own backyard. Following our excursion from Avignon, Cousin Kim and I nearly exhausted ourselves with a few days of buying frenzy, when we at last declared ourselves "shopped out."

During one particularly hectic arm-laden-with-shopping-bags afternoon, as we lingered over a two-hour lunch of asparagus risotto accompanied by a fine white wine, life couldn't have been more perfect. The sun warms our backs, we're free of the kids for a few hours, and we located some clothes that actually fit.

Earlier in the day as I browsed in one boutique, I noticed the dressing room curtains billowing and desperate grunting noises sounded from behind the thick velvet drapes. Rather reminiscent of the Wizard behind the curtain on the classic movie, "The Wizard of Oz." I pulled back the curtains only to discover cousin Kim trapped in a pair of pants. I advised her to remain calm as I tried to extricate her from the sausage casing. I calmly tell her my sister, Shannon, experienced the same fate with a similar style of pants while at a Christmas party. I didn't tell her that Shannon eventually lost the battle and had to rip her pants. At this point the saleswoman appears, I ask her in my best pronoun laden/first person verbiage French for the largest pair of pants in the boutique and a pair of pliers. She shakes her head in the negative while her sides heave with ill-disguised mirth. In America, everything is super-sized, even the people. Not so much in France.

At another boutique, Kim tries to retain her composure, as I emerge from the dressing room in a fetching brown linen suede-belted jumpsuit. After Kim stopped laughing and cleaned the slobber off of her face, she inquired about my oversized buttocks. Only someone who's known you all of your life can ask such a question. I can only conclude that the French sizing isn't compatible with American figures and this American is way too fond of the *pain au chocolat* or small croissant filled with dark chocolate.

Tomorrow we head to the Cinque Terre in Italy where it's rumored the people and clothing are sized a bit larger.

Cinque Terre, Italy

This week, Leslie and I toured the Cinque Terre in Italy with cousin, Kim, her two girls, and her husband, Greg, who recently joined us from the States. Craig and the boys are spending spring vacation in Seattle. The boys are homesick for their friends, Craig has business matters that need his attention, and we need more Jif Peanut Butter, Kraft Macaroni and Cheese and Starbucks coffee.

Ciao, pronto, buon giorno, and *arrivederci*, this is the extent of my vocabulary while traveling in Italy. I often lapse into French as a fallback from my four words; it's just too difficult to move from speaking French to Italian. The Italians ignore my French unless they are very old. The older Italians learned French as a second language in school, while the younger Italians learned English as a second language.

We traveled by Eurail quite efficiently. Kim is in charge of the train schedules, while I'm in charge of the savages (the three kids) and Greg is the pack mule, or "donkey boy" as we fondly call him.

The Cinque Terre, Italy is an unspoiled smaller scale French Riviera with hiking trails connecting the towns. Americans are traveling again after the tragedy of 9/11; I honestly hadn't seen more than ten American tourists since we arrived in France.

I'm now tired of seeing my fellow Americans. They're easy to spot. Eddie Bauer backpacks, hiking boots for the trail along the Cinque Terre, and of course, Rick Steve's guidebooks complement each khaki-clad American. As a Euro local, I try to blend in. Who wouldn't wear a leather jacket and clogs to hike the Cinque Terre? Although, I admit the clogs aren't the best choice for footwear and hiking the trails. I lagged far behind my tennis shoe-wearing relatives as I stumbled up and down the treacherous trails. Little nine-year old Leslie skipped ahead of me, never noticing the precipitous drop to the crashing waves and jagged rocks down below. This did nothing for my fear of heights.

Americans filled the first restaurant on our stop; each head was bent over Rick Steve's Italy travel book. This is culture shock, listening to voices I can actually understand. While touring the Cinque Terre, we stayed in La Spezia, a quaint little town with a notable naval museum, and commuted back and forth by train to the various towns. This area isn't to be missed!

After visiting the Cinque Terre, we headed for the train station to catch a ride to Siena. While running through the train station, I notice I'm missing one of the savages. My niece, seven-year old Dakota, isn't following behind me as instructed. The other two girls are right on my heels while Kim and Greg are busy trying to figure out the train schedule. Panic ensues. Not only is it time to catch the train, but the platform is very crowded. Remembering Cody is a "shopper," I head for the nearest trinket shop. Most likely, she's drooling over a shiny keychain or just looking at the European candy she can't get in the States. On my way to the souvenir shop, I spotted two small feet underneath an enclosed phone booth. Sure enough, the holey little shoes belonged to Cody, who is pushing every button and unsuccessfully hunting for spare change. Cursing Cody under my breath again, we sprint to the train, which is now pulling away.

While touring the circular city of Siena, we hiked everywhere. Kim and I lagged far behind, pausing to gape at each boutique window. Yet another ancient city with a medieval heritage, Siena has three districts that all meet at the glorious Piazza del Campo. While sipping a very strong espresso in the piazza, we learned that Siena is the home of the annual Palio Horse Race, held each year on the 2nd of July. The plaza is encircled by boutiques and cafés. Alas, we arrive on a Sunday and all the shops are closed.

Greg thoughtfully occupies the savages the following day while Kim and I dash from shop to shop during our allotted free time. We're overjoyed to discover the Italian clothes aren't sized for Barbie dolls but for "real people." I hear no frantic sounds from the dressing room as Kim tries on one outfit after another. Yet again, I have occasion to regret wearing my clogs as we trek through the cobbled streets of Siena. Enticing lemon-colored cashmere scarves peek out of one boutique, while a rolling rack with soft leather coats stands in front of another shop. I score an enormous, fabulous canvas bag, the design on the front covered in sequins. Perfect for hauling my purchases—fashionable and practical. I'll be sorry to leave this very navigable, enticing city.

Our next stop is Citadella Del Capo, Italy. My niece, Madison, has been communicating with a pen pal in the village of Citadella for most of the school year. Her third grade teacher at St. Francis spent six months in Florence as a young college student. She maintained her friendships in Italy, one who is the third grade teacher in Citadella Del Capo.

Madison's entire class from St. Francis had written letters for the Italian third grade class, which Madison delivers in person to the local Catholic school. She carries her brown paper sack full of letters from her classmates into the classroom of expectant students and suddenly grows shy as she is introduced to the third grade class in addition to all of the other grades, a daunting experience for any third grader. The Italian children ask such fascinating questions in their best English such as; "What time is it?" and "What is your phone number?" and my all-time favorite, "What is your favorite color?" Grades first through third are attired with little black smocks over uniforms; apparently, this distinguishes them as the younger children.

Our hostess (the third grade teacher) is extremely generous with her time. We visit the theatre (she had the keys,) and then the Sprint factory, which makes road bikes (she had the keys.) Kim and I are hopeful for the keys to the various enticing boutiques, but she walks right past the stores. Lunch is waiting for us at the third grade teacher's home, which I mistake for an art gallery due to all of the antique paintings and treasures. Fortunately, I didn't ask the price of anything and disgrace our group. After lunch, we toured more sights, until they all began to run together.

The third grade teacher is indefatigable, more sights and more lectures the next day. My attention wanders as the rain steadily increases, and we have no umbrella. Lord, this is turning into a nightmare, Kim is very crabby and leaves it to Greg to chat with the Italian schoolteacher as she extols about the merits of her small village. Of course, we also meet all of the third grade teacher's friends and relatives. The Italians are by nature very generous and welcoming, I hope the teacher didn't witness Kim's glazed over eyes.

Ready to relax after the whirlwind tour of Citadella, we hopped on the train again for the northern part of Italy, the lakes district, made famous by Bellagio and Lake Como and the well-known off and on ex-pat, George Clooney.

Our base for several days is the small village of Verona, at a small three-star hotel. The hotel landlord has an efficient yet unusual manner of operating her hotel. After our evening meal, the light above the table turns off, leaving us no choice but to leave the dining room. Sometimes the light flickers a bit before we finish, and we bolt our food before she clears the plates from the table. Electricity is expensive in Italy and France, however, this shutting off of lights seems a bit abrupt. Five minutes of hot water per person is available at the hotel only in the early morning and early evening. I very nearly disgraced myself when I turned on the spigot for my bath and cold water spilled forth. Marching down the stairs and mentally calculating how much more the 4-star hotel is going to cost, I discovered from another guest that hot water exists but only at certain times of the day. Military showers do have their advantages; however, they aren't to my liking.

Bellagio is picture-postcard perfect with the snow capped mountains in the background. At the moment the lakes are choppy, and there's no George sighting, dashing about on his speedboat. The ferries are used for transportation in this neck of the woods; it's not advisable to miss the ferry, as there aren't a lot of other options available. Once again, sainted Greg takes the girls on an adventure while Kim and I explore the waterfront sights and shops. When we eventually find Greg at a small park, he's talking to a man from Bellevue, Washington, a city fifteen minutes from Seattle.

Back at the hotel we linger (until the lights flicker) over one last delectable Italian meal and head off to bed before the lights in our room shut off also.

Upon returning to France, Kim and Greg prepare for their trip home. I retreat to my outdoor laundry line, away from the hustle and bustle of packing. A perfect vista of the valley lies below me, groves of olive trees and crumbling old stone houses dot the valley. The sun is out, the lemon tree in the yard is in full bloom, and the birds are singing. I'm in paradise, which will be disrupted tomorrow when my two rambunctious boys and their father return from "across the pond," as the Brits like to say.

More Tennis

Well, our time is quickly ending here in our little piece of paradise, but perhaps this isn't such a bad thing, because Craig and I are nearly crippled from taking lessons with the relentless Philipe. We started tennis lessons in January 2002. Craig progresses nicely with his game; he lobs, volleys, and smashes overheads with apparent ease. I, on the other hand, concentrate on moving the cement blocks posing as my feet, and simply returning the ball within the boundaries of the tennis court. Despite these hindrances, I enjoy myself immensely because Phillipe, the tennis instructor is very handsome. I enjoy the game too, of course.

Today, Craig, our oldest son, Austin, also known as "happy son" due to his early onset of puberty and I thought we would get a bit of exercise and play a quick set. Playing tennis with three people is difficult at best and "happy son" soon becomes "sulky son" when he has to sit out for too long.

As we warmed up, I perhaps used my swat technique a few times. Craig of course, notices this and comments on my form. Not only does he mention my rather unorthodox tennis style, but he advances to the net to show me the appropriate stroke (Craig's stroke) and how to perfect it, demeaning me in front of "happy son" (now "laughing son") and of course, the people on the opposite court. I quietly explain that I have an instructor and could he (Craig) manage to play a game without feeling the need to give me instructions. He continues to correct me. I pack up my racket and march off.

I find my friend, Laurie, who owns the club with her husband. She's entirely sympathetic to my plight because she too has a know-it-all, bossy husband. We commiserate over some tea while joyously watching Craig hit ball after ball high in the air (sky-balls due to bad karma.) I'm also secretly thrilled I no longer have to play with "happy son" who is growing dangerously close to having zero partners due to his unsportsmanlike-like behavior.

Tomorrow we leave for the island of Elba, (the kids have yet another break) where "happy, sulking, laughing, son" will have the opportunity to practice more of his erratic teenage behavior at the resort.

Oh, How We Love the Italians

Isola d'Elba, is off the coast of Sardinia. We love the Italians, so happy and friendly, welcoming and willing to help a weary traveler. So unlike some of the French, dour with perpetual frowns, we make exceptions for the wonderful French people in our library group in Grasse, *trés gentil* (very kind).

While traveling to Elba, Austin places himself in the shotgun seat of the car. I assume he knows this position in the Ferrari of Minivans necessitates an ability to navigate. As I while away my time in the backseat, reading magazines and looking out the window, Austin points out the "hot" cars and extols over the giant yachts lazily cruising the blue seas of the Mediterranean. Craig, unable to get Austin's attention, reads the ketchup-stained and crumpled map. Austin tries unsuccessfully to refold the map back to its original pristine form. Seeing the hopelessness of this task, he concludes that the map is defective and can't be refolded.

We finally arrived at our first overnight stop without the help of our navigator, Austin. At the Hotel Royal, the kids make a tremendous fuss over the heated swimming pool, much to the locals' dismay. Not only are they noisy, but the other hotel guests loudly worry the kids will catch pneumonia. However, the Italians love children almost as much as the French love their dogs, it's only Craig and I who shout at the kids to be quiet—always a good technique to shout at children who pay no attention. The other sun-bathers soak up the sun through intermittent clouds, wearing long pants and sweaters. Tomorrow we continue our journey to Elba via train.

Parking the car at the train station, we begin our four-hour journey to Campiglia, Italy. Somehow we scored a compartment all to ourselves, well almost. There is one man in the two-benched compartment. I notice he leaves the area frequently. When I put myself in his shoes, I would have done the same. It's not pleasant to listen to the incessant chattering, bickering, and farting that characterize our kids. They're savages, apparently not quite so cute to this particular Italian. Once the long train tour ends, we find our way to the ferry, where we depart to our final destination, the island of Elba and the Hotel Hermitage.

Arising the next morning, we're all eager to explore the postage stamp island where Napoleon lived as the resident exile. Napoleon was a *"Corse"* from the island of Corsica and maintained a much-admired estate on the island. His very short bed remains in the bedroom with his other miniaturized furniture, sort of like a hobbit hole, but on a much grander scale.

While driving around the island of Elba, Craig takes pride in his attempt at driving as the local Italians do. He passed any and all vehicles he deems unworthy. Passing the garbage truck on a blind corner remains a bone of contention for us to this day. The boys are stoutly on his side, "Dad had to pass, we would have been following that guy all day." No matter, Craig is fired (by me) from the driver position after that little maneuver for the safety of the passengers. I may be slow, but at least we arrive back at the hotel in one piece.

Later at the hotel, we agree to play a game of tennis doubles with Conner and Austin. Leslie is relegated to ball chaser and water girl. I play with Conner who is always a good sport. I nearly perfect the spin on my swat. My mother says the trick is to let the wrist go totally loose and then flick the ball at the opponent, not knowing where it will land. My trick worked during this particular game because I received no complaints from my fellow players.

After a rousing game of tennis, we troop into dinner. The waiter is so gracious; he proudly presents us with an English version of the Italian menu. Nothing is too good for us, as he hovers anxiously. "Do we enjoy our foods?" What are you kidding? The food in Italy is only to be rivaled by the food in France, but in France, it's more difficult to enjoy a meal with the stiff atmosphere that permeates some restaurants. Certainly, no one would ever think to ask if we liked our food. The French believe in leaving the diner alone, which of course means no service.

Traveling by rental car, ferry, and train back to France takes its toll on all of us. With each stop we make, it's apparent we're getting closer to France. Grim-faced passengers board and replace smiling passengers and the laughter all but ceases on the train. Our arrival in Nice, France is a somber event—we grow tired of each other and look forward to our own beds.

School started the following day and with it the talk of the approaching Spring *Fête* and the Father/Son basketball tournament. This causes great consternation among the fathers—they're willing to do most anything to get their title back. Practice (for the dads) commenced immediately after school.

• • •

Craig's Observations on Italy

You can smile in Italy and not be deemed a fool. For the first (and only) time, Shawn described something accurately. After our trip to Italy last week, my first to this wonderful country, I get it. The Italians are some of the friendliest people on earth, they have mouth-watering food and wine, and their countryside is stunning. In France, if you walk down the street with a smile, you are considered mentally deficient. In Italy, if you don't walk down the street with a smile, you must be from France. We spent four days on Elba at a secluded resort in a small cove on a sandy beach. The headwaiter, upon learning we were Americans, had the menus translated into English for dinner on the following evening. There were many exotic choices, and I was happy that the children tried some new things. Conner stepped up and ordered Loin of Rabbit, but pronounced it Lion of Rabbit. The waiter did not flinch. Maybe the Italians have a new breed of predator rabbit, I don't know.

I love the way the Italians drive, fast and furious. It's what you would expect from a country that produces Ferraris and Maseratis. The phenomenon extends beyond the owners of these fine roadsters; however, drivers in tiny Fiats and garbage trucks drive fast too. We toured the island one morning in a rented Fiat Punto, a car for five, but a more accurate capacity is 3.5. We were following an RV and another small car on a classic winding road along the sea (cliff to the sea with no guardrail) when a garbage truck approached quickly from the rear. Garbage must have a short shelf life in Italy, as the driver started honking his horn and proceeded to pass me on a curve with limited visibility. He rounded the next curve on two wheels, honked again, and proceeded to pass both the sedan and the RV in one shot. These drivers pulled off to the side, I believe to change their underwear, so we followed Mario Garbagetti for the next few kilometers, but finally I had to give up the chase. He was just too fast for the Punto.

• • •

Visitors

Craig's sister and brother-in-law will arrive soon from the States. I'm overjoyed to have someone else to talk to after our little family's last excursion to Italy.

I arrived home from *Le Champion* with my groceries to find our guests have already arrived. I'm mildly surprised to see them here so early because our home is difficult to find and the rental car agency at the airport is nearly impossible to locate. They plan on staying with us for a week.

As I park my minivan, I gently touch the bumper of their car with my van. Perhaps it made a small noise, I don't know. As I attempt to park my car again, Craig, who is easily rattled, runs out of the house, arms waving and shouting all sorts of things.

I couldn't hear him because my radio is turned up to a particularly good song. He insists on parking my car as my relatives stare at their auto in dismay. I must say they maneuvered their car in such a way in the driveway that it was nearly impossible to park another car. All of this commotion produces a huge smile from Levio, the first I've witnessed—in seven months thus far.

After the car-parking incident, my thoroughly dismayed brother and sister-in-law head off to the grocery. This isn't unusual for them, they're well-seasoned travelers and want to have a look about while it's still daylight. Craig and I neglect to let them in on the shopping-cart-release-secret. This is a rather mean-spirited game Craig and I play with all the new arriving guests.

We're perversely curious to see if it takes other non-local people as long as it took us to release the shopping cart from its chained prison. I recall it took us, Rick, and Shannon a half an hour to figure out the intricacies of the shopping cart release at Carrefour.

They return a short hour later and when asked, Nan and Bob said, "It only took us fifteen minutes to figure out the cart, an old lady came over and helped us." For some reason, this is mildly annoying to me. I'd bet my bottom dollar that some choice words were exchanged before the old lady helped them.

Nan and Bob have very little trouble adjusting to life in France. They seamlessly move in, cook occasional dinners, and explore the countryside with us.

St. Tropez

Surprisingly, Bob is overly eager to visit any town with the possibility of visiting movie stars. The tiny town of St. Tropez is a two-hour drive from Grasse but well worth the visit.

St. Tropez, on the Côte d'Azur, started as a meeting place for artists and still has the feel of an artist's community, as evidenced by the specialized cobbler in the old town St. Tropez. My southern friend, Susan insisted. "*Yew* must *gooo* visit that quaint little *stowah* and get some leather sandals made for *yew*." Susan is pretty reliable for knowing these sorts of things so of course I must have my feet fitted for the hand-made thong-like leather sandals. For some reason, I'm the only one in our group of four who wants the leather Jesus sandals. I'm sure the others will be sorry later on.

The city is surprisingly empty of tourists and stars alike. It's even difficult to find an open restaurant for lunch. The resort town really comes alive at the end of May and closer to the Cannes Film Festival, when the stars and other wannabes come out of the woodwork and make the little town their own.

Nan and Bob pride themselves on walking everywhere, and so we hiked high over the town of St. Tropez to the Citadel, built between 1590 and 1607.

Bob is still anxious for some star sightings and I promised to take him into Cannes for the film festival before he leaves. I guess reading the *Star* and *Enquirer* doesn't satiate his desire to see the rich and famous.

• • •

Craig's Observations on the Minivan

Our return to France from Italy was without incident. Unfortunately, Shawn put another notch in her belt to mark the fourth car she dented since arriving in France. Recall she dented our first minivan last September when "big onions fell off a truck and bounced off my hood;" she dented her sister's car, "I thought I could make the corner;" she dented our second minivan, " I thought I could get by his bumper;" and a few days ago she and added a new set of dents to our second minivan, "I accidentally gently touched their bumper." Not exactly. The true story follows: I heard her coming up the driveway, so I went to help her carry in the groceries. I looked through the window and saw her nudge my sister's car, but she kept going until it was almost on two wheels. She backed up a little, then proceeds to follow the exact course and bumped the car again. I guess she was absent on a critical day in high school geometry when arc and radius were discussed. At that point, I very calmly raised both arms, giving her a signal to halt the progress of the vehicle before she ripped the rear door off the minivan and her rear bumper off the other car. Luckily the dents on the minivan are in the same location as the previous dents, which I grudgingly admit, takes some skill. I apologized to my sister and told her the first fifteen minutes of her stay with us would not, in any way, resemble her experiences over the next four days. I overheard her later calling around in search of available hotel rooms, but it's the Cannes Film Festival, so she had to stick it out at our house. She wisely parked her car on the far end of the property and rolled large rocks around the perimeter of the car as a barrier to any other possible mishaps.

•••

Report from the Cannes Film Festival

We are taking in the local festival today . . . the Cannes Film Festival, hoping to see movie stars and stargazers acting like fools trying to get noticed. I'm sure this doesn't apply to us.

Craig's sister and brother-in-law, Bob and Nan are still here. Bob has a thing for Sharon Stone and hopes to catch her eye with a new practiced come-hither look. I asked him to show me his "look" as we drove to the train station. He declined. Finally we're becoming very practiced at train travel, which is quite useful in the busier spring months on the Riviera. Shannon and Rick decide to accompany us also.

The smiling faces of Nicole Kidman and Tom Cruise greet us from mammoth billboards when we walk into town from the train. A lot of tourists and paparazzi mill about the area but no stars, at least no one I recognize. After an hour of standing around, I'm feeling frustrated and cheated. Here I am at the Cannes Film Festival and my only celebrity sighting remains a paper-plastered billboard of Tom and Nicole.

Craig is ready to head back along with his sister and brother-in-law, when we notice an excited group of expectant-looking people. Of course, I immediately walk over and start asking questions. "*Qui attendez vous?*" or (Who you wait for?) Grammatically incorrect as usual, it's clear they understand me; however, no one answers. Maybe they don't know. Shannon and I wait with them, determined that "someone important" will show.

It's incredibly hot, and Shannon has sweat dripping down her face. I feel it's my duty to tell my sister her extremely "dewy face" isn't a good look for the camera. Just then a reporter steps into the small crowd to gather interviews. Perhaps I shouted a few garbled French phrases at him, I don't remember, but my very American accent gave me away and he interviewed me for his Dutch television station. My sister says I acted like a total idiot. Jealousy doesn't become her.

As a giant limousine pulls up the curb, David Lynch climbs out with a "How y'all doing?" Much applause although I have no idea who he is until Shannon tells me. I'm just about to give up hope when another limo pulls in to the curb. Sharon Stone arises from the shiny black car, much like the goddess Aphrodite, and strikes a pose. The peace sign she flashes enthralls the waiting group of paparazzi and looky-loos, (Bob) She has a rather stilted demeanor, but what do I know about these things? Having thoroughly, although briefly assessed her outfit, I decided that her statue-like posture is a result of having to keep her very casual shawl sitting "just so" on her shoulder. One false move and the silky shawl floats to the ground. She looks fabulous in a low-cut, apple red blouse with suede pants.

Bob has a most embarrassing habit of foaming at the mouth when his darkest thoughts get the best of him. I'm afraid that Ms. Stone is having this effect on him. Having no bib, and wanting to spare Nan any further embarrassment, we head home in the early evening by train.

Once at home, I immediately called my southern friend, Susan, because none of my people will attend the Cannes Film Festival with me again tomorrow. Thank goodness, she wants to attend the festival. "Perfect, maaah friend, Cathy, is here, she'll love it," says Susan.

It's a funny thing about the various visitors to our little piece of heaven from the United States. Our small group of friends in the area "share" visitors. It's an exciting event when a guest comes for a stay from the States. None of us are completely fluent in French and crave additional company and news from across the pond. Hence, Susan's friend, Cathy, is immediately my new dear friend also. I hope she (Cathy) is aware of this.

Film Festival Repeat

The following day, once Susan, Cathy (my new best-friend), and I are offloaded from the train, we walk toward the already crowded waterfront, Boulevard de la Croisette, where the *fête* is taking place. We make a beeline for the small groups of people, figuring I had good fortune the previous day with this method. Lots of people watching, locals dressed as mimes, a fellow hanging on a cross on the beachfront, a menagerie of sights, but alas not a celebrity in view. Susan, ever the great communicator, engages a friendly security guard in conversation. It appears that a few celebrities are going to come in from their private yachts. What luck!

Soon enough the security guard mumbles into his speaker, which is cleverly hooked to the collar of his shirt collar, and Debra Messing steps off the skiff, high heels and all. Not a practical boating shoe but what a great look! Her gorgeous red-tinted locks fit right in with all of the pink-and scarlet-haired locals in the area. Following Debra, who, by the way, is very friendly to the few of us who are gathered at this secret spot, is Johnny Depp.

Susan nearly faints with pleasure. She shouts hysterically, "Johnny, you're my man." He doesn't give any indication he heard her as he has his picture taken with a little girl. Susan is crushed by his supposed curt dismissal of her; however, our friend, Cathy, has other plans. As Johnny makes his way to the waiting limousines, Cathy flings herself onto the hood of his car, narrowly escaping being run over by Johnny's limo driver. She obtained a window-tinted picture of Johnny for her distraught friend.

We drag Susan away from the departing limo, and have the good fortune to run into my old friend, Sharon Stone again. My esteem has jumped substantially for Ms. Stone because of rumors that Ms. Stone recently had a brain tumor removed. No wonder she has on a large floppy hat, which does nothing for her long floral grunge-like peasant dress. The look is simply not good for her. From my up close view, it's clear she isn't wearing make-up and she still looks fabulous. Curse her!

After the star sighting trifecta, we all headed home and regaled Craig with our many stories. He missed out today. Cathy and Susan join us for dinner where we entertain Craig with embellished details of our personal experiences with the celebrities.

Now in country now for nine months, we've yet to visit Paris. Actually, I'm a bit nervous to visit Paris; the Parisians have an entirely different accent than the people in the south of France. Decidedly, they'll have no tolerance for Craig's hand signals.

Paris

We hired a nanny for our out-of-town trip this time; we can't burden Crystal with our three rambunctious children again. During our stay on the right bank in Paris, we stay at a hotel a step up from the crumbling pension I stayed in as a student in the spring of 1977.

The crowds at The Palace of Versailles aren't manageable. None of us wants to wait with the masses of people to shuffle from room to room like a moving herd of cattle. But we do anyway. The tourist season is in full swing at Versailles. After the Maldives, the four of us are used to more "civilized travel," we aren't accustomed to lines and the pushing and shoving. The Americans, Japanese, and the Germans fill the courtyard at Versailles. We manage to enter the palace where we're shoved and pushed from room to room. The French tour guide behind our group constantly interrupts our English-speaking guide to complain about the slowness of our group. It's true our guide seems to exhibit signs of ADD; he's distracted by anything and everything. The entire palace trip is very disjointed, and I remember very little except being constantly trod upon by other tourists. It's a huge relief to finally be pushed outside.

In the gardens surrounding the palace, music is piped in from somewhere, and plays in time to the spouting fountains. Rather picturesque in a Las Vegas sort of way. Both my sister and I have a love for all things planted, although Craig claims anything green at my home eventually wilts and dies from neglect.

Shannon and I are in dire need of a restroom; Rick suggests that we eat lunch in the restaurant at Versailles. Simply using the restroom in the restaurant without ordering food isn't acceptable in France. Surprisingly, the waiter is very efficient, in the past we've waited fifteen to twenty minutes before a waiter even approached our table. Perhaps the waiter is too efficient, as he clears the table while shouting wildly over our heads before we finished our food. As the server neatly pushes us out the door, another waiter knocks into me with a hot plate of food. During lunch, Shannon and I lobby for a carriage ride through the gardens, much to our husbands' dismay. Much eye rolling takes place between our husbands when we climb in the horse-drawn carriage. The tour guide drives so poorly I have a neck ache by the time we exit the horrid carriage ride. The driver, perhaps feeling bad about tossing his hapless passengers about in the buggy or wanting a tip, advises us to visit the Petit Trianon before we leave the grounds.

Marie Antoinette commissioned this special petite country home to escape from the palace and court. At the mini palace there is a small farm for her animals and a mini thatched cottage for the children, really charming, and the best part of Versailles.

In hindsight, I should have listened to my cousin, Greg, who advised us to completely skip Versailles, but like the lemmings we sometimes are, we neglected to follow his advice. Tomorrow we go on a tour of Normandy, a two-hour car ride from Paris.

Normandy is incredibly humbling and awe-inspiring. To see the different areas off the cliff where the Americans, Canadians, and British landed is unbelievable. Imaging that anyone was able to scale the terribly steep cliffs, in full army gear while being shot at is difficult to fathom. Once the soldiers landed, they were sitting ducks, as the Germans shot at them from the well-sheltered dugouts. Omaha is a level beach, but the tide was very low when the troops landed, forcing the soldiers to run a long distance before they could find any cover.

After we toured the cliffs, the surrounding area, and the memorials, we watched movies in the Normandy Museum dedicated to D-day; these movies portrayed actual footage, giving the viewer a very powerful sense of what occurred.

Lunch after the tour left something to be desired—yet another experience with a hostile waiter. The French waiters in the museum cafeteria are positively beastly. The tour guide doesn't notice the rude staff and gives us dining instructions. We should've paid more attention to his cafeteria tour.

It's long past the lunch hour, even for France. I notice a serving table off in the corner with a few silver-covered platters and several plates at the end of the table. I can't help myself—I'm starving. I dart over to the table, and help myself to some mashed potatoes and the accompanying brownish meaty looking stuff. A kitchen person accosts me. She charges through the kitchen door almost as if she has been lying in wait for me, maybe there is a peephole. The hostile hostess grabs my plate out of my hands and shouts something at me while gesticulating to the other foul looking food. Now I'm not a picky eater, but I can see food-poison written all over this particular dish she wants me to eat. In the nicest way possible, I convey that I prefer the nice brown goulash and potatoes. "*Je mange des pommes de terre.*" (I eat potatoes.) She says in English, and I quote: "NO, it is finished." I relay (in English) that I'm very happy with my mess of brown and potatoes and make a dash for my table before she grabs my plate from me. At the table, Rick is sitting silently with potatoes and the nasty goulash the kitchen hag tried to shove onto my plate; he doesn't have the strength to talk about the reincarnated kitchen Nazi. Witnessing my disaster with the wench, Craig and Shannon opt to eat leftover breakfast baguette for lunch.

Despite the lunchroom fiasco, we all immensely enjoyed Normandy and the D-day tour, a proud day to be an American.

On our return back to Paris, there's an extra passenger in the 4-wheel drive vehicle. He is rather large and reeks of some sort of French onion, his mass covers a full half of the front car seat, thus leaving me uncomfortably close to the driver. Hopefully he (the driver not the large man) won't get the wrong idea. The drive back to Paris seems to take a long time.

Tomorrow we tour the Museum D' Orsay and several shopping districts in Paris.

Europe is littered with great history and great painters; we are very fortunate to see the works of Monet, Manet, and Cézanne the today at the Museum D' Orsay. A fair amount of Monet's garden scenes were painted right in his backyard. On a more morbid note, we visited one particular gallery that had nothing but photographs of dead people. I'm not sure what that photographer thinking.

Shannon and I insisted on a boat ride down the river Seine, which is very picturesque, but perhaps we should've hired an English-speaking guide to fully understand the lecture. We did recognize the Notre Dame from the river.

At the end of the boat ride, after listening to Shannon and me discuss a shopping excursion, Rick and Craig abruptly leave us after lunch. Parisians love to eat and they love to enjoy a LONG lunch, during which time the shops are closed. Shannon and I wandered aimlessly around looking for some shop, any shop that's open. We happened upon a Gap store, and Shannon darts into the store. After I forcibly drag her out of the store with, "Who shops at Gap in Paris?" she grows peevish. I ignore her and continue window-shopping.

A store featuring lingerie-like clothing beckons me. Lingerie boutiques are almost as plentiful as *boulangeries* in France. At the filmy fabric store, a sweet little blouse with cats on it catches my fancy. Shannon scoffs, she knows I don't like cats, but at least I'm not shopping at The Gap. I buy it anyway.

In the evening, we attend the Moulin Rouge, a provocative show of women wearing nothing but pasties and feathers. This troupe of "barely-there" women dances the Can Can, as they flaunt their feathers, and expose their jeweled g-strings. As I clean the spittle off of Craig's tie, I wonder about the eating habits of the waif dancers. These French women don't have any flesh on them whatsoever, although apparently Craig and Rick appreciate their skeletal forms. I console myself with the thought that the dancing girls feathered clothing hangs on them like sacks, however, I resolve to go on a diet just as soon as I return to my home in Grasse. This may pose a problem, as I've yet to find anything labeled "low fat" or "no fat" in the Champion grocery store, I decide to think about it another day.

Our Final Visitor

Our year-long sabbatical in France is quickly coming to an end. When I look back, I'm happy I've kept a journal because all of the small stories and events that consume our day-to-day life are what make the trip come to life on paper. Talking to the kids during dinner about our various side trips and their new friends, I also detect a hint of sadness from them. I know they will bring back the memories of our family vacations from our home base in France, and hopefully are humbled a bit by being the kid who speaks one language (and a bit of French) instead of the three or four that the other school children speak. I know they look forward to our final visitor from the states; she has kids their age at home and brings news from their parochial school.

Jay, my book club friend, is here from the United States. She says she's only staying three or four days. Doubtless, she'll opt to stay longer just as all of our other guests have. The Grasse valley is brilliant at this time of year.

Jay arrives bringing me the most recent, *Star, National Enquirer*, and *The Seattle Post-Intelligencer*. She says she donned a disguise in order to purchase the illicit material; as a fellow book club member, she isn't impressed with my choice of reading material. However, after gawking at all the celebrities during the Cannes Film Festival in May, I'm very interested in the paparazzi pictures.

Jay says she wants to relax while she's here. She's currently "relaxing" while taking a brisk walk in the ninety degree heat, our ideas of relaxing are somewhat different. Jay also says she doesn't want to be in charge; I'm happy to boss another person around in my household. My children stopped listening to me long ago, and this gives me ample opportunity to practice my bossy skills.

Today, Jay, Susan, Shannon, and Susan's visitor, and I visited the Isle St. Honorat, a short ferry ride from Cannes. Isle St. Honorat is currently the home to thirty Cistercian monks, and its main attraction is a monastery where the thirty monks still practice. Part of the monastery is open as a gift shop where the monks sell their homemade honey and monastic goods. As we explored the church, we're careful not to intrude on the few monks at prayer. One particularly old fellow wanders over to us, and I can't help but notice his feet and hands are immense. He points his cane at us with his gnarled hand and treats us to the most beatific smile I've ever witnessed. I immediately resolve to be a monk in my next life. To be so at peace or at least appear to be is a wonderful thing.

It's a sunny day as we wander around the island; most of the monastery is closed to visitors. Being a natural spy and a bit curious about "monkly life," I unsurprisingly, want to penetrate the "inner sanctums" of the monastery. A hole in the wire fence is too small for my growing girth. We come across a giant stone wall, which Jay encourages me to scale, but again my pencil arms can't pull up my wide bottom. Outside of the monastery, we spy a group of male picnickers. One fellow doesn't appear to have on any pants. This is somewhat titillating but I don't explore any further. Perhaps my imagination is getting away from me, yet again.

After a leisurely sun-soaked day, we regretfully take the ferry back to Cannes where I must face the inevitable task of thinking of something to make for dinner. Somehow, I'm never able to escape this chore. Craig is a haphazard chef at best.

Jay is very enthused about playing tennis with Philipe. I guess Americans don't mind being shouted at when on vacation, and of course, he is handsome. She is currently perfecting her version of the swat, which I have down to a patented swing. My mother and cousin are quite good at the swat also. During my last lesson, Philipe told me, "Get off the court." I've decided to take this as a compliment.

Sadly, my friend leaves tomorrow; she accomplished her sole goal —relaxing.

Austin is home from a school-sponsored rock-climbing field trip. He claims he had a great time but said the food was bad and he got no sleep. The only American in a tent of Italians; the Italians amused themselves by pelting small stones at each other every night before settling down to sleep. Must be a Euro thing or more likely just a boy thing. I unpacked Austin's bag when he failed to do so after numerous requests, a fortunate thing as I noticed flies swarming by the foul parcel. Some very suspect "reading" material with a lot of pictures stares me in the face, as I unzip the bag. He has the grace to look embarrassed when I question him about his choice of magazine. After discussing the illicit reading material with Craig, we decide to write it off as an "international boy thing."

We settled back to enjoy our remaining three weeks in France when our plans change drastically.

∾ Part VII ∾

In the End

The Uninvited Guests

Craig and Austin came home after basketball practice completely knackered. I had dinner waiting for them and listened with rapt attention to Craig's game plan for the following weekend. Once again, it involved shoving the young bucks around and hoping for a shot. I diverted the conversation to our past nine months in Grasse, France.

Looking back, I'd have done a few things differently. For one thing, my children would be allowed no food from home, in particular processed cheese—a much sought after commodity by the neighborhood kids and a few tastebud-challenged adults. No Kraft Macaroni and Cheese, no Cheez Whiz, and certainly no Velveeta. However, our three young children continued to pine for their preservative filled cheeses and so my husband dutifully brought back suitcases full of the stuff each time he made a business trip to the States. Our home became known as warehouse for all those cheeses that required no expiration date.

One evening, the six of us were just sitting down to dinner at 7:30. The phone rang and Conner expecting it to be one of his many friends, jumped up to answer it. The phone is located on the kitchen counter and a window immediately opposite the counter has a view of the parking pad, one story below. As Conner spoke with the neighbor child (and yes he did want some Velveeta), he tried to smother his voice while turning away to the window. *"Oui, oui,* my dad just brought back ten boxes of Kraft from the States. What's the Gameboy game called? I'll trade you five boxes for Junkfest Zombies."

"Conner that's it, get off the phone and quit bartering the food your dad brought back from the states.

Conner's response wasn't quite what I expected.

"Robbers, robbers," shouted Conner.

"I mean it, Conner! This has gone far enough! Now sit down and finish your carbonara."

However, as he continued to leap about shouting, "Robbers," we all got up and looked out the window. Unfortunately, he was correct, six men in dark clothes wore what looked like "Zorro" eye masks, and seeing us spot them— sprinted to the back of the house. The rear of the house is the only section of our nearly impenetrable fortress of a home that has a possible entrance. Clearly, the invaders had cased our home before.

Leaping the low iron fence, one after another and quickly smashing the glass of the back French door, they were nearly in the house. Craig, being a take-charge type of guy immediately shouted instructions to the rest of the family as he made intimidating gestures to the robbers. They were intent on capturing the six of us (my niece was visiting) and didn't waiver from their goal. At that time, their intentions were still unclear to us.

Our boys, Austin and Conner herded, Leslie and Kylie upstairs into our master bedroom. They had the presence of mind to grab a fire poker, kitchen knife, and golf club to use as possible weapons. I on the other hand—dithered. There was no other word for it. Should I join my children upstairs within the safe confines of the panic room or stick it out with my husband? Craig did not then nor does he ever dither. He shouted at me to run upstairs. I did, but not before two of the robbers caught up with me. One held my arm and put a gun to my head while the other shouted at my son, Austin, in a heavily accented French, *"Ouvrez la porte (Open the door)."* The intruder continued to point the gun at my head as I shouted over him, "Close the door, Austin, close the door." Austin assessed the situation quite calmly and shut the door. I was done dithering but was now being held captive by the intruders.

It briefly crossed my befuddled brain that at one time I thought the Benums crazy to have installed a steel door to their bedroom, which doubled as the panic room. Clearly, they had prepared for the worst and the kids were going to test out the safety of the room first.

I was forcibly dragged downstairs to Conner's bedroom and thrown onto Conner's unmade bed. I had time for a flicker of annoyance that Conner hadn't cleaned his room, but perhaps he hadn't anticipated the gunmen. Nevertheless, I made a mental note to give him a strongly worded lecture. Three of the six gunman were in a heated discussion.

"C'est femme de l'épicerie de Champion, prendre ses bagues." (She is the one from the Champion grocery, take her rings.) In the frenzy of the situation, my ear, now well-trained in the French language heard . . . "She has a ring of cheese from the Champion grocery." Simple enough, I thought, but why would they go to all this trouble for a ring of cheese? And what was a ring of cheese?

"You, my good fellow, can have all the rare American boxed cheese you want, we have an entire garage full of boxed cheese, though I regret we're fresh out of rings of cheese." This is what I wanted to say, but what I think I actually said was: *"Vous fromage de chèvre."* (You goat cheese.) This didn't go over well.

The three masked robbers grew very red in the face leading me to suspect a potential language miscommunication. Fortunately, there was an interruption in the "conversation."

Craig was manhandled into the room and thrown on the bed beside me. It was apparent he'd been in some sort of tussle. Blood dripped down the side of his face and he cradled one bruised hand to his chest.

"What do they want?" asked Craig.

"I think they said they wanted a ring of cheese."

"What? That can't be right! Well, just give them what they want for God's sake!" Said Craig

"I'm trying to tell them where to find the cheese."

Craig, now desperate, began a complicated series of hand gestures made even more ridiculous by the lack of an international hand signal for "cheese." Things weren't looking good for us, and worse yet, the gunman appeared to have noticed a safe in Conner's closet.

"Ouvrez le coffre-fort." (Open the safe.) The gunman was now extremely annoyed with me, he starts waving his gun around and making the gesture for "looney tunes" while pointing at me.

"Craig, I think they want some coffee with the cheese." *Coffre* sounded enough like the word coffee to me but I didn't understand what coffee had to do with the safe.

"Pourquoi la femme de cet idiot contiue-t-elle a parler du fromage et du café?" (Why does this idiot women continue to speak about cheese and the coffee?) The gunman asked no one in particular.

I calmly explained in English that the coffee was upstairs in the pantry. They silently looked at Craig and I and pointed the gun in our direction. I watched the gun move back and forth, from my forehead to Craig's forehead, *à la* Russian roulette. This was awful, I couldn't understand their French and they couldn't understand my French. Craig asked them if they spoke English, because clearly neither my impeccable French nor Craig's international hand gestures were adequate communication.

I'm not even sure that they were French. I didn't recognize their accents. At this point one of the gunmen, frustrated and angry with us, hit Craig in the head with the gun. For what it's worth, Craig can now say that he has been "pistol whipped." The "pistol whipping" caused the gun to fire in a single deafening blast. I looked at Craig and said quite calmly, "Don't worry, Craig, I'm sure the gun is full of blanks."

By the startled looks on the gunman's face, it was apparent he didn't know the gun was loaded. A light went off in my muddled brain; they wanted us to open the safe! They don't want cheese or coffee, they want money and jewelry. One of them grabbed my hand and forcibly removed one of my rings. The other ring wouldn't budge off my baguette-plumped finger.

Yet another masked man burst into the tiny room and said he couldn't get through the door of the panic room where the four children had barricaded themselves. At least I think that's what he said because he pointed to the ceiling while shaking his head several times and my ears were ringing from the gunfire. He brought a roll of duct tape and proceeded to wrap us together by the hands, and feet. All that was needed was the pole to hang us upside down like two trussed hogs on the way to the spit.

Because the robbers couldn't cut the phone wires, which are housed in a metal box outside, they knew the kids were most likely calling for help. I picked up a few random words from their discussion, though I may have invented their exchange to make myself feel better.

Meanwhile in the safe room . . . the four kids formulated a plan. The steel door to our bedroom held strong despite vigorous kicks, thus giving the kids ample time to plan an escape. They phoned the police and our immediate neighbor. The police said they would be over later. Not an uncommon response when they know weapons are involved. The police don't carry firearms in France. In the unlikely event the robbers managed to break through the steel door, the kids planned to climb out the window, shimmy down the olive tree, and make a run for it.

The robbers finally realized their well-planned robbery had gone awry. With Craig and I now duct taped together, their parting words were, "Do not move." They must have rehearsed those words before they came, because we never heard them utter another English word. We waited perhaps a minute before we started struggling with the tape.

After listening to Conner's pleas for help over the phone, our British neighbor is galvanized into action. After making sure that his own family was safe, he raced over to our home—armed with a shovel. He literally charged through the now open garage door while brandishing his shovel. Craig, still dragging duct tape from his foot grabbed a rake and raced through the olive orchard with the neighbor to get a good look at the possible getaway car. "They have guns, and you have a rake, it's not a garden party, wait for the police." I shouted. Naturally, I was a bit agitated due to the fact that I nearly had my head blown off.

"You poopheads, cowards, meanies." I could hear the kids' screams and shouts from the master bedroom window as they watched the home invaders run across the olive orchard. I ran upstairs and alerted my brave little soldiers that we were safe. "Did they find the cheese, mom?" asked Conner.

"No Conner, your American cheese is safe." No sense in letting him in on the real horrors of the episode downstairs.

"Mom, we climbed out the window onto the roof, the robbers were getting pretty close to kicking in the door," Austin told us.

I phoned Shannon, knowing I would need her to help me speak with the *gendarme* (police). She arrived quicker than the *gendarme* and I briefed her on the particulars. Craig began to practice his hand signals in case Shannon's

French was insufficient.

Two *gendarmes* finally arrived, along with a rather handsome detective. Because Craig had a head injury sustained by a pistol whipping, they called in a doctor. Thirty minutes later six *gendarmes*, one doctor, and the chief detective were all at the house. The detective questioned us (in English) intently while surveying the scene of the crime. "Were the men carrying guns?" the detective asked us. "Yes, I saw several guns, but I'm not sure everyone had a gun." At this point, the detective pulled aside his long overcoat and pointed to the largest handgun I'd ever seen. "Did it look like this?" What was he doing carrying a gun? None of the other gendarmes appeared to be carrying weapons. "I don't know, it's all a blur," I said.

"Are you hurt?" said the detective. "No, I'm not hurt, it's my husband, he has a gash in his head and his ears are ringing from the gunshot." Monsieur Detective grew very animated at the word "gunshot." "Gunshot, where?" he asked. "Here in this room, the bullet is probably in the wall somewhere." Suddenly, the room is filled with most of the *gendarmes* looking for the stray bullet.

The detective was elated when he discovered the bullet of the misfired gun in the wall. It seems to me that bullets are usually used as evidence; this bullet was left upstairs on the kitchen counter, but only after having been passed around the room and rolled in the fingers of the thoughtful detective and his cronies. Perhaps they left it as a souvenir for us.

When they left, they requested that we go in to the police station the following day to fill out yet another report. No response from either Craig or me. We had already experienced a visit to the Police Station when Craig was run over while riding his bike earlier in our trip. Neither of us could abide a trip back to fill out yet more forms with no apparent follow-up from anyone.

The next day the story was all over Grasse and the French Riviera, in the newspaper and on the radio. Our fifteen seconds, or, I should say thirty minutes of fame in the worst way possible. All of us were traumatized and none of us felt safe in our home. We decided after a family vote to return home to the States. The kids had only three weeks of school left.

"You'll miss the spring *fête* and the dad versus seniors basketball tournament." I said. All the while I'm thinking that I escape the parent "volunteer" duties associated with the spring *fête*.

"Can we stay at Aunt Shannon and Uncle Rick's house until we leave?" asked Leslie.

"Of course, I'm sure they'd be glad to have us, and Licky will be there to protect you." At this point she needed all of the support we could give her.

After months of preparing for our journey to France, it only took three days to pack up our possessions and secure flights home to Seattle. The kids were celebrities for a few days at The International School though visibly distraught at leaving all of their new-found friends. Conner received numerous phone calls each night, no doubt trying to trade our stockpile of cheeses for some new gadget.

We informed the Headmaster of the International School of Nice of our early departure. She was shocked at the violence of the home invasion and supportive of our decision to leave France early. The kids received the marks they currently had in school. Hopefully, Conner finished his last project.

In Retrospect

Despite our rather unorthodox ending in France, we truly enjoyed ourselves. There's a lot to be learned from living abroad, good and bad, but in our case mostly positive.

Occasionally bashing the French and their customs served as good humor around the dinner table but the French for the most part were generous, warm people. Craig and I experienced genuine concern from the local French people when, first Craig was involved in the bicycle accident and then, we were the victims of an unheard of crime in the south of France. On a more trivial note, here are a few other things that we took home with us:

1. The roundabouts—The Americans really need to adopt this method to circumnavigate traffic at intersections.
2. The lack of after school activities and the slower pace of life in general. It's nice to get off of the merry-go-round of constant after school carpooling and six day a week practices.
3. The closure of stores from 1:00-4:00, forcing people to relax and not run about doing one chore after another all day long, although it would have been nice if there was at least one 24-hour grocery store open.
4. The clothesline behind my house, not only a "green" way to dry the laundry but a soothing activity to boot.
5. New friends all experiencing the same thing and having different crazy adventures trying to adjust to a new culture.
6. The food. I left France twelve pounds heavier even though I rode my bike everyday and exercised with Philipe like a fiend. I never figured out how to eat like a local and stay thin.

In retrospect, here's what I would do differently:

1. I now NEVER EVER travel with expensive jewelry. It was later reported that the robbers had been scoping out jewelry-clad people in the Champion grocery store and following them home. My escape was a lucky one; the woman up the street had her finger cut off in order to procure her expensive ring.
2. I would have joined the neighborhood clubs earlier in our stay to meet people who had things in common with us.
3. Research the safety of the area where I planned to live. At least

one-fourth of our friends were victims of some type of crime in the south of France.

4. Bring half of the clothing that we brought. Wearing American-made clothing makes you even more obvious as a foreigner.

5. Use the Eurail system more frequently, we only got the hang of the train system in the spring when our trip was almost half over.

6. Eat half as much food.

7. Become proficient in the language of the country I plan to live in *before* I arrive. In hindsight, I acknowledge that while American cheese, and particularly Kraft Macaroni and Cheese, was a favorite of my children, it proved a dreadful contributing factor (because of my inability to interpret the intruder's language) to the almost disaster of the home invasion.

Every single day was an adventure and one that I would not trade for the world. We are a stronger, tighter family because we experienced life in the slow lane and one small misfortune together.

About the Author

Shawn Underwood grew up in Bellevue, Washington, where she attended an all girls Catholic school. Given the choice to attend a public or private high school, Shawn chose public school, whereupon her parents replied "wrong choice." It was the smartest decision she never made since at the time, her fondest desire was to live in a commune. After graduating, Shawn attended Washington State University, earning a B.A. in Speech and a Graduate Degree in Audiology—fields that proved to be particularly useless in her future endeavors as a humor writer.

Over the years Shawn held a wide variety of jobs, which provided excellent fodder for her writing, but maybe not excellent wages. She failed to make her mark as a strawberry picker due to her languid picking style and flipping burgers left her feeling greasy. Shawn also worked as an "under" maid to the rich and famous in a resort town where she served appetizers at secret service-staffed cocktail parties and picked up the dirty underclothes of important people.

Fortunately, she did eventually find her true calling. Shawn is currently the humor columnist for her local online newspaper, *www.b-townblog.com,* where she poses as "Underwood—Undercover." Thus far, her celebrity status as the only humor columnist in town has garnered neither free dinners at her favorite restaurants nor slashed tires. Shawn also contributes to *www. nightsandweekends.com,* a website that reviews movies, books, and music. Her short stories are featured in the "Instant Gratification" humor column.

One of Shawn's short stories, "Mom Versus Computer" was included in two 2009 anthologies: *People of Few Words— Fifty Writers From the Writers' Showcase of the Short Humor Site,* published by Lulu, and in *Laugh Your Shorts Off: Short Stories to Make You Giggle* by Award Winning Authors," published by CreateSpace.

While living in France Shawn discovered just how much she enjoyed humorous lifestyle travel writing. Since then, Shawn has been documenting her extensive travels on her website, *www.ShawnUnderwood.com*. Shawn's first book, *Mommy, Are We French Yet*, was published in 2010 by Five Star Misadventures.

These days Shawn divides her time between her "office" in the neighborhood Starbucks, (the only place she can concentrate on her writing), her three children, two poorly behaved Cavalier King Charles Spaniels, known as Mr. Big and Mr. Small, her long-suffering husband of thirty years, and her Red Cross volunteer duties.

Visit Shawn's website and sign-up for her blog reports
about more of her travel adventures.
www.ShawnUnderwood.com